Lord, Give Me Patience,
and Give It to Me Right Now!

JAMES W. MOORE
BOB J. MOORE

LORD,
GIVE
ME
PATIENCE!

... AND
GIVE IT
TO ME
RIGHT
NOW!

Abingdon Press
NASHVILLE

LORD, GIVE ME PATIENCE, AND GIVE IT TO ME RIGHT NOW!

Library of Congress Cataloging-in-Publication Data

Moore, James W. (James Wendell), 1938–
Lord, give me patience and give it to me right now! / James W. Moore and Bob J. Moore
    p. cm.
    ISBN 978-1-4267-0760-5 (binding: pbk./trade pbk., adhesive - perfect : alk. paper)   1. Christian life—Methodist authors.   I. Moore, Bob J.   II. Title.
    BV4501.3.M66423   2010
    248.4'87—dc22

2010001316

10 11 12 13 14 15 16 17 18 19—10 9 8 7 6 5 4 3 2 1
MANUFACTURED IN THE UNITED STATES OF AMERICA

To the most important people in my life:
June, my beloved wife and soul mate; and our family,
Jodi, Danny, Sarah, Paul, Jeff, Claire, Dawson,
Daniel, and Mason

—Jim Moore

To Cynthia, the love of my life and my greatest
supporter; and to our family, Wendell, Bettina,
Caroline, Kelsey, Preston, Cissy, Ed, Jim, and Christian

—Bob Moore

CONTENTS

INTRODUCTION

Lord, give me patience, and give it to me right now."
This is actually a pretty good prayer. When we see
this prayer on signs or billboards or bumper stickers or
lapel buttons or stuck on the front of somebody's re-
frigerator, it may cause us to smile quietly or chuckle
out loud or speak out knowingly about how we relate
to it, but the truth is that it's a prayer we all need to pray
often. The prayer may convey images like these:

- A young mom pushing the hair out of her face as
  she cleans up after her three preschool children
  who have just scribbled on the dining room walls
  with their new crayons and magic markers
- A business executive ready to make an important
  presentation to a key prospective client when tech-
  nical difficulties come to call
- A couple preparing for a fun dinner party when,
  just as the guests begin to arrive, the couple drops
  the casserole on the kitchen floor
- An office worker who is having a "Murphy's Law"
  day where whatever can go wrong does go wrong

- And they are all praying the same prayer, "Lord, give me patience, and give it to me right now!"

Now, we can all nod our heads with understanding because we have known firsthand those kinds of difficult days and those kinds of trying experiences. The truth is that, along with "patience," there are many other things we need from God. There is much help we need from God, and that is what this book is about: God's gracious availability to be with us and God's amazing power to help us in any and all circumstances. So, this is a good prayer to pray today and every day: "Lord, give me patience and love and grace. Lord, give me faith and forgiveness and resurrection. Lord, give me the abundant and meaningful life that can come only from your generous and merciful hands, through Christ our Savior. Amen."

There are so many gifts we need from God. This book will mention only a few of them. We know you will think of others, and we hope you do.

On a personal note, I want to say how pleased I am to have the privilege of writing this book with my big brother, Bob, who over the years has always been a great brother, a great friend, a great counselor—and a great inspiration to me.

CHAPTER ONE

Lord, Give Me Patience

SCRIPTURE: MARK 10:17-22

S ome years ago, a noted senator was asked what was the single most difficult aspect of being a United States senator. His answer was interesting. He said the hardest thing to deal with was the frustrating fact that his constituents back home had a "bad case of the simples!" That is, they expected him to work instant miracles in Washington.

They so easily reduced all complexities to neat little black and white simplicities. He said they didn't seem to realize that the most meaningful and significant accomplishments take time, effort, commitment, sacrifice, discipline, perseverance, and patience.

In a sense, this was the rich young ruler's problem. When he came to Jesus in search of real life, in search of something to fill the inner emptiness gnawing at him, in search of something to satisfy that deep hunger in his soul, he wanted no complicated personal involvement. He wanted an easy answer, an instant miracle, a simple solution. But when Jesus told him that this was no simple matter—that this is a life commitment that touches all that you have and all that you are—impatiently, the rich young man turned away sorrowfully because he wanted a fast, easy, simple remedy—a quick fix.

Remember the story with me. Jesus has set his face toward Jerusalem. He is on his way to the Holy City, on his way to the cross. This is serious business now. He is thinking deep thoughts when the rich young ruler runs up and kneels before him and asks about eternal life.

There are some fascinating things to notice here. This man is a rich *young* ruler—that is, he has all the things we (in our world) so openly long for—wealth, youth, power. Some would say, "He has it made! He has it all—wealth, youth, power. What more could he want?" But you see, that is precisely the point. Despite having all those things, something is missing in his life. He knows it, he feels it, he senses it. Something is missing! There is a void, a vacuum, an emptiness, a hunger that is not satisfied, a thirst that is not quenched.

Money, power, youthfulness—wonderful as they are—are not enough. Something more is needed to make his life full. He knows that his life is incomplete, so he comes to Jesus in search of a quick and simple solution. After all, he is probably used to getting exactly what he wants, simply and quickly. He is a "ruler."

When he speaks, people are quick to say, "Yes, sir." When he calls, people jump and come immediately. When he wants something, people rush to "step and fetch it."

Now, although we are not rich young rulers, that mindset is not alien to us. In a sense, we have become a spoiled people who are impatient with delays, detours, or even disciplines. We want things done for us quickly and simply. The *push* button has become our symbol. Why wait or work for anything? J. Wallace Hamilton in his book *Serendipity* put it like this:

> *"Pay one dollar down. Get it now!"* *"Clothes cleaned—one hour."* *"Cars washed—two minutes."* [We] . . . itch for the instantaneous—instant coffee, instant biscuits, instant cereal, . . . [instant credit, instant e-mail, instant faxes]. We are impatient people . . . looking for near ways, short cuts, quick results, simple solutions . . . [and usually we want somebody else to do it for us]. (Westwood, N.J.: Fleming H. Revell, 1965, 158)

I'm thinking of the family planning a vacation who

says, "We should go to London this summer. Call our travel agent. She will make all the arrangements." Or the businessman buzzing his secretary on the intercom and saying, "Wedding anniversary coming up this weekend. Pick out something nice for my wife and have it sent out." Or the children who break their new toy and say with a ho-hum shrug of the shoulders, "It's okay—Daddy can get us another one."

In something of a similar vein, the rich young ruler may have approached Jesus that day asking for eternal life because when Jesus shows him the cost of discipleship, the commitment demanded, the effort, the change, the risk, the personal involvement, the sacrifice that touches even the pocketbook, the young man is disappointed and he turns away, trudges away, misses his moment because he wants a religious quick fix rather than a total life commitment.

The point is clear: the things that matter most in life do not come quickly, easily, or simply. Not long ago, I read about a new car owner who called an auto manufacturer. He said, "Was it your company that announced that you recently put a car together from start to finish in seven minutes?" "That's right! We did it," said the executive proudly. "We put a car together from start to finish in just seven minutes." To which the caller said, "Well, I just want you to know, I think I have that car!"

The things that matter most take time, effort, patience, sacrifice, discipline, and deep commitment. Too much, too soon, too easily—is the perfect formula for frustration, heartache, and mediocrity. When we get too easily and reach too quickly, we tend to appreciate too lightly. To be sure, some things you can get immediately by pushing buttons or paying money down or by pulling out a plastic card. But the great things, the real values, do not come that way; they have to be grown and cultivated. You can get a sports car or a flat-screen TV with a quick down payment, but character, morality, integrity, maturity, spiritual strength—these you have to wait for, work for, want intensely, commit to, and cultivate and grow slowly but surely.

Sometimes our children's choirs sing an anthem called "Little By Little." It has this significant line in it: "Good things that are here to stay, don't get done in just one day."

The rich young ruler just didn't understand that being a disciple is no simple matter, that becoming spiritually mature is not instant or easy. It is costly! But it is a greater treasure by far than anything we have ever known. Let me illustrate the point further by looking with you at three things that we really need to work at and commit ourselves to if we are to attain any measure of spiritual maturity and understanding.

1. First, There Is Prayer

Developing a meaningful prayer life is no simple matter. It takes time and effort and energy. It takes practice. It takes patience.

Not long ago, I was watching a late-night TV talk show. The host was interviewing a man whose name you would recognize immediately if I were to state it. He is known all over the world as one of the greatest golfers of all time. He is a world-famous sports figure. He made an interesting confession on TV that night. He said, "I have never been what you'd call a real church-going Christian, but I do consider myself a religious man. When I was a little kid (four years old), my mother taught me a bedtime prayer, and I still say that same prayer today. It's the only one I know."

You know, that seemed kind of sad to me because that is not what happened in other areas of his life. As he grew older and stronger, he did not continue to play golf as he did when he was a "little kid." I should say not! Through hard work, practice, effort, discipline, sacrifice, and commitment, he became one of the superstar golfers in the history of sports. He became one of the finest athletes to ever walk on the face of the earth. But at the age of fifty-two, he is still repeating the same prayer he learned as a child of four. His prayer life had never grown, never stretched, never matured. It was static. There was no development at all. There is something disheartening about that, isn't there?

But who are we to throw stones at him? Most of us are in the same boat. Speaking of boats and prayer, remember the story about the two men caught in a small rowboat in the midst of a storm. As the waves rose higher and the boat threatened to capsize, the men knew that they needed help. They decided prayer was their only hope. So in the teeth of the gale, one of them shouted, "O God, you know that I haven't bothered you for the past fifteen years, and if you'll just get us out of this mess, I promise you I won't bother you again for another fifteen years!" Somehow that fellow had missed the point of what prayer is all about, hadn't he?

When all is said and done, the real question with regard to a good prayer life is: Do we really want a good relationship with God? Do we really want a strong friendship with God? Do we want it so much that we will work at it diligently and consistently and persistently for as long as it takes? Simply put, prayer is friendship with God and healthy friendships take time to develop. They need to be nourished and cultivated and celebrated until they become as natural and as comfortable as breathing. Strong friendships don't happen overnight. They have to be worked at.

If you want to become a doctor, lawyer, minister, teacher, musician, an architect, engineer, or athlete, it takes determination. You have to plug away at it. It doesn't come easily or simply or overnight. Maybe the same thing is true with prayer. Maybe it takes a lot of practice and a lot of patience.

2. Think Next of the Scriptures

Developing a meaningful understanding of the Scriptures is no simple matter. The truth is that while the Bible is in nearly all of our homes, not all of us are at home in the Bible. How is it with you? Do you feel at home with the Scriptures? Is the Bible a friend or a stranger to you? When crisis comes, you need a friend. In desperation people have turned to the Bible for strength, for comfort, for the word of life, expecting instant simple solutions, and sometimes they have come up empty because they didn't know how to find its treasures.

Edward Blair, in his book *The Bible and You*, points out:

> The person who is looking for a way to master the Bible in three easy lessons will be disappointed. In the first place, one can never master the Bible. One can only be mastered by it. In the second place, the Bible is so immeasurably rich that the human mind cannot possibly embrace it all in a few attempts. Familiarity with the

Bible comes only by long exposure to its contents. (Nashville: Abingdon Press, 1953, 52)

I know a minister who does an interesting thing. In preparing for funeral services, he takes the Bible of the deceased person and skims through it to see what has been marked or underscored or written in the margin. He says he discovers a lot about the person from his or her Bible. Interesting, isn't it? And it raises a good question: What would your Bible say about you?

3. Finally, Think about the Church

Being a real, committed church person is no simple matter. Becoming a real, devoted church person is a growing, developing thing. It is not a single act or event. It is not one experience suddenly over and done with. It is a process, a pilgrimage, a life commitment.

The initial salvation experience, however it may come and however wonderful it may be, is only the beginning; there is much to follow. It's like a wedding. It is easy to have a beautiful wedding, but it takes a lot of work and commitment and love to make a beautiful marriage.

I am convinced that many professing Christians do not understand this. They have the simplistic idea that when they have "accepted Christ" and joined the church, that's all there is and there's nothing more. They see this initial experience as the final goal when really it is only the starting place. They think they have graduated when really they have barely enrolled. It is a wonderful thing to become "newborn," to become a "babe in Christ," but to remain a spiritual baby is tragic. Babies are sweet and adorable, but if they remain infants and never grow up, we consider that a calamity, and it is.

Ernest Hemingway, the superb storyteller, won the Nobel Prize for Literature in 1954. His novel, *The Old Man and the Sea*, was cited. It's the story of an old man, a Cuban fisherman, who for eighty-four days had gone without a catch. On the eighty-fifth day, he went a bit farther and caught a giant marlin. It was a great struggle to land the prize catch. It took three days, but finally the old man, with his hands torn and bleeding, his body aching with pain, won the battle. He had caught the fish. He couldn't get the huge fish into his boat so he lashed the eighteen-foot marlin to his boat and headed for home, thrilled with his victory. But then the sharks came and feasted on his catch. When the old fisherman landed in his harbor, all that was left of his magnificent catch was a skeleton. His great earlier victory ended in heartbreaking defeat.

When we look around, we see the sad fact that this happens to so many people in their faith experience— they end up with only a skeleton of some earlier victory.

Like the rich young ruler, they came to the Master, realizing that he has the answer to life. They have a warm and brief encounter with him, but then unable to make the rest of the journey, they turn away sorrowfully because they want a simple, easy solution.

The truth is, it's no simple matter. When it comes to real faith, and real discipleship, we need a lasting, tenacious commitment—to prayer, to the study of the Scripture, and to the church.

As God makes us over, God does it in his own good time, and more often than not it takes awhile. As Bishop Hazen Werner put it some years ago, there are "no saints suddenly." Each of us as a Christian is a work in progress. So, a good prayer for us to pray today is, "Lord, give me patience . . . and please give it to me right now."

CHAPTER TWO

Lord, Give Me Faith

SCRIPTURE: LUKE 8:49-56

It all started on a Sunday afternoon in the month of May. Our father quite suddenly became terribly ill with a ruptured appendix. I was twelve years old at the time. I had never before seen my father sick. He was always hale and hearty and healthy, the strength of the family. He was rushed to the hospital. My brother, age fourteen; my sister, age six; and I stayed at home with our grandmother and waited anxiously for some word. About an hour or so later, the chaplain from Methodist Hospital, Bill O'Donnell (who had formerly been our pastor), knocked on our front door. He told us that we should come with him because both of our parents were injured in a car accident and had been admitted to the hospital.

We went to the hospital, but we couldn't find out much—just that our mother was being cared for in the emergency room and that our father was in surgery. We walked the floor at the hospital and prayed in the chapel for several hours before we were sent home for the night.

Shortly after my brother, my sister, and I had fallen asleep, the call came from the hospital that our father had died. Even though I was only twelve, I have several vivid images of that tragic event in our lives. First, when the call came about my father's death, the relatives who had gathered in decided to let the children sleep. They felt it would be best to let us get a good night's rest, and then tell us the bad news in the morning. But what they didn't count on was that I got up early and went out to get the morning paper. When I opened it up, there on the front page was the picture of our smashed-up car, and the caption beneath announced that my dad had died in the car wreck.

Before anyone could tell me, I read it in the newspaper. I remember as if it were yesterday, sitting in the living room of our home early that Monday morning with the newspaper spread across my lap and the relatives coming in and seeing me and not knowing what to say. And I remember even in my shock and grief feeling sorry for them.

Another vivid image that would change my life forever came that night at the funeral home. As we stood there by my dad's casket, hundreds of people came by—all different kinds of people. Some were rich, some were poor, some were young, and some were old. Some were African Americans, some were Anglo Americans, some were Asian Americans, some were Latin Americans, some were professional people, some were uneducated laborers, some were unemployed, some I knew quite well, and some I had never seen before. But they all came. They came over and spoke to us and expressed their sympathy—and every one of them said the same thing to me: "Jim, your dad was kind to me."

Now, they didn't all use those exact words, but each one in his or her own way said the same thing: "Jim, your dad was kind to me." Even though I was just twelve years old at the time, I made up my mind then and there that the best tribute I could pay to my dad was to take up his torch of kindness, to somehow with the help of God let his kindness live on in me, to keep his special brand of kindness alive and well in the world through me, to pass his kindness on to everybody I meet—and from that moment I have tried my best to be a kind person. There are a lot of things I'm not, but since that day I have tried, as a tribute to my earthly father and my heavenly Father, to be a kind person. I haven't always succeeded, but I have tried and I am still trying to let my father's kindness live on in me. You see, I know what kindness is because Wendell Moore was my father! And I have learned even more what kindness is because Jesus Christ is my Savior. The best tribute I can pay my dad and the best tribute I can pay my Christ is to keep their spirit of kindness alive and well in this world. In similar fashion, the daughter of Jairus would have been able to say later in her life: "I know what great faith is because Jairus was my father."

In Luke 8 we find Jairus's story. Jairus was the ruler of the synagogue, so his family represented the upper crust of society. He was a man of substance—rich, powerful, and religiously prominent.

In the synagogue, he called the shots. He decided who would preach, what scriptures would be read, and what hymns would be sung. He represented the elite of society, especially in the religious world; and given his position, he probably would not normally have given much time or thought to this traveling teacher from Nazareth called Jesus.

But crisis came. The angel of death hovered over Jairus's house. Jairus's twelve-year-old daughter was critically ill. It looked hopeless. She was dying. As Jairus stared the potential death of his daughter in the eye, he became a different man. He became a desperate man.

He swallowed his pride. He pushed the rules aside and he ran to Jesus for help!

Let me put a footnote here. By this time, many of the synagogues were closed to Jesus; many religious leaders were suspicious of him. They didn't want to be associated with Jesus because so many of them saw him as an untrained troublemaker who was upsetting the people.

Jairus may well have been one of those doubting detractors, but then his twelve-year-old daughter was dying. So Jairus (loving father that he was) threw caution to the wind and ran to Jesus for help! He fell down at the feet of Jesus and pleaded with the Master to come to his house, because his only daughter was gravely ill and dying. Jesus went with him. He healed a sick woman along the way. And then messengers came from Jairus' house telling him that his daughter had died. "It's too late. All over. She's gone. No need to trouble the Master anymore." But Jesus, on hearing this, says to him: "Don't be afraid. Just believe and she will be made well."

They go on to the house. The people are weeping and mourning. They scoff at Jesus for even thinking he can do anything about this. But Jesus goes to that little girl and he resurrects her. He loves her back to life and then (I love this), he tells them to give her something to eat.

Now, of course, there are many beautiful lessons in this powerful story in Luke 8, but for now let's look closely at the faith of this father. Three things stand out.

1. First of All, His Faith Was Active

There is a fascinating story about a naïve villager who was born and reared in a remote, obscure, rural community. One day he traveled to the big village for the first time. He obtained lodging at an inn, and during the night was awakened by the loud beating of drums. He asked what all the drum beating was about. He was told that it meant a fire had broken out in the village and the beating of the drums was the city's fire alarm.

When he got back home, he quickly told the village leaders about what he had learned in the big village. "They have a wonderful and effective system in the big city. When a fire breaks out, the people beat their drums, and before long the fire goes out."

Well, as you can imagine, this excited the village authorities greatly. So they ordered a large supply of drums and distributed them to the people. When a fire broke out, there was a deafening sound of drums beating everywhere. The villagers anxiously beat their drums and waited for the flames to die down and go out, but to their surprise and dismay, the fire did not go out and there was much destruction. About that time a sophisticated traveler from the big village was passing through. "What's going on?" he asked. When he was told how they had beat their drums and beat their drums and still the fire had not gone out, he said, "Oh, no! You misunderstood. Do you really think a fire could be put out by beating drums? The drums don't put out the fire. They only sound the alarm for the people to wake up and to take action to fight the fire and extinguish the flames."

This is a valuable parable for those of us in the church who think that the beating of the religious drums of ritual and rhetoric will solve our social ills or bring healing to our troubled world. It's not enough to just beat the drums; we have to actively do something. The weepers and wailers had come to Jairus's house to mourn the death of Jairus' daughter. This was a part of their culture. Professional weepers came to cry loudly, to play mournful-sounding flutes, and to tear their garments as signs of respect for the one who was dead or dying. But Jairus could not content himself with that. He sprang into action. He ran to get help. He ran to bring the Great Physician there to heal his daughter.

The point is clear. The Christian faith is not just a creed we profess; it is a lifestyle we actively practice. It's not enough to beat the drums or talk a good game. We have to walk the walk and actively live the faith. Jairus's faith was strong that day because it was active.

2. Second, His Faith Was Hopeful

Everybody else had caved in and given up, but Jairus would not quit. He kept on hoping, and he placed his hope in the right one.

During the Great Depression, a group of leaders gathered in Chicago to address the burdensome problems facing the people of our nation. These leaders went to an African American church on the South Side of Chicago. People from the neighborhood came in to discuss their woes and problems as they tried to survive the Great Depression—no jobs, little money, big bills, sagging morale.

Among the leaders who went to see how they might help were a prominent theologian and a famous agnostic attorney. The attorney decided to take advantage of the situation to dramatically underscore the plight of African Americans. He said to them, "You have no jobs; you have no money; you have no power; you have no opportunity." And then ended by saying, "And yet you sing. No one can sing like you do! There's something I don't understand and I want to ask you about it. What in the world do you have to sing about?"

There was silence in the room, and then the voice of an elderly African American woman came from somewhere in the back of the hall: "We've got Jesus to sing about!" Oh, yes, we have lots of problems, but we also have Jesus and he is what we sing about. For once in his life, the attorney was stopped dead in his tracks. He was face-to-face with people who had faith and hope in Jesus.

If you and I could somehow get into a time machine and go back to that scene in Jairus's house in the first century, we would probably hear the people saying something like this to Jairus: "It's hopeless, Jairus. We've done all we can. It's no use. We're so sorry, but all hope is gone." I can just hear Jairus answering, "No! Jesus is near. He can help. He can bring healing. He is our hope."

That's the good news of our faith, isn't it? We can always be people of hope because Jesus is near. We've got Jesus to sing about.

Jairus expressed a great faith that day because he refused to quit; he refused to give up. First, his faith was active, and second, his faith was hopeful.

3. Third and Finally, His Faith Was Trusting

Even after word came to Jairus that his daughter had died, he kept on trusting Jesus.

One of the warmest memories of my childhood was something that happened to me when I was five years old. I had spent the day with my grandmother. Toward evening, a fierce storm hit. "Oh, Jim," my grandmother said. "How in the world are we going to get you home in this weather?" The answer came moments later as my dad walked in the front door. He had come to get me.

The storm showed no signs of letting up. The wind was blowing hard, rain was pelting down, lightning was flashing in the sky, thunder was rumbling behind the clouds. It was a dark and scary night. We didn't have far to go to get to our house, but the storm was nasty and getting worse. My dad had on a big, navy blue, all-weather coat, and as we got ready to leave my grandmother's home, he said, "Jim, come under here." He covered me with his coat, he picked me up, and out into the storm we went.

Even though it was raining hard and the wind was howling and I couldn't see a thing under that coat, I was not afraid at all. Why? Because I knew my father could see where we were going. So I just held on tightly and trusted him. Soon the coat opened and we were safely home.

Death is like that for the Christian. Grief is like that. The problems and challenges of life are like that too for the Christian. God covers us with his protective love. He holds us up and guides us through the storm. Sometimes in this life there is no way around it. We have to walk through the pain, the storms, the heartache. But the good news of the Christian's faith is this: we never walk alone. God is with us and he will see us through.

Jairus knew that, and that's why he had a great faith—a faith that was active, a faith that was hopeful, and a faith that trusted Christ. That's the kind of faith we all need, isn't it? So this is a good prayer to pray today: "Lord, give me faith and please give it to me right now."

CHAPTER THREE

Lord, Give Me Life

SCRIPTURE: LUKE 19:1-10

Some years ago, a *Ziggy* cartoon showed Ziggy walking past a store window. In the window was a large sign that read: "Eat Yogurt—add years to your life." To which Ziggy said, "If it would add life to my years, I'd be interested."

This is a great parable for us and it is precisely what the Zacchaeus story in Luke 19 is all about. Zacchaeus knows that something is missing from his life. There is an emptiness, a vacuum, a gnawing hunger deep down in his soul. Even though he has become a wealthy man through his shady tax collecting practices, he is not happy. He is unsatisfied and unfulfilled. He is thirsting for something more, so he comes to Jesus looking for the answer and he finds it, or better put: Jesus finds him!

What a great and memorable story this is! It's a brief story about a man's encounter with Jesus, but it dramatizes the good news of the Christian faith. It reveals dramatically the Gospel's openness to all sorts and kinds of people, and especially its impact on a life and on a community. And it demonstrates the meaning of Jesus' mission statement in Luke, "I have come to seek and save the lost."

But what really makes it a great story is its relevance to our time, and the images of ourselves and those we know that can be found in the life of this man, Zacchaeus. We see the image of those who are willing to sacrifice everything relational to get ahead, to be a success, to achieve position, power, and wealth. The story also reflects how meaningless and unfulfilling this kind of achievement can be.

In Zacchaeus we discover the kind of restlessness that many of us have in our lives, that haunting feeling that causes some to cry out: "Is this all there is?" Zacchaeus found that even when he got all that he thought he wanted, it did not bring him happiness or a sense of really being alive. Many others have made this same discovery.

His venture to see Jesus was really a search for meaning and a search for life. He must have wanted it desperately, because he took the risk of being ridiculed and climbed up into a tree to get a glimpse of Jesus.

What was it that attracted Jesus to him? What was it that made Jesus stop in his tracks and interrupt his journey to Jerusalem to spend some time with Zacchaeus, a tax collector and outcast in the people's eyes? Was it the incongruity of a grown man up a tree? Was it perhaps his vulnerability out on a limb? Was it the beginning of humility to go to such lengths to encounter Jesus? Or was it the quiet desperation in his face or the lack of life in his eyes?

We don't know what Jesus saw when he looked at Zacchaeus, but evidently, when Zacchaeus looked into the encouraging eyes of Jesus, he saw the new life he could have; he saw the new Zacchaeus he could become; he saw the Zacchaeus he was meant to be. We are not sure what all happened there. We don't have all the intricate details, but we do know that Jesus stopped, Jesus invited, and Zacchaeus responded. We don't know what they discussed in Zacchaeus's home; we only know that Zacchaeus was dramatically changed in his attitude, lifestyle, morality, generosity, and in his care for others.

In the Gospel of John, Jesus expresses his mission statement and purpose: "I have come that you might have life and have it abundantly." That's what this story is all about: in Jesus, Zacchaeus found life and found it abundantly.

Isn't that what Zacchaeus was looking for? And isn't that what we are looking for? Wouldn't you like to not only add years to your life but also life to your years? Zacchaeus wanted to really live before he died, and I have a feeling that many of us can relate to that. That's why the Zacchaeus story is so important to us. Zacchaeus's encounter with Jesus underscores the ingredients needed to add life to our years.

1. First of All, to Add Life to Our Years, We Need a Healthy Relationship with God

It is crucial to have a spiritual dimension in our lives, a vital connection with the divine, or more simply put, a personal relationship with God through Jesus Christ.

Zacchaeus realized that something was missing in his life. For all that he had achieved and accomplished, he still felt unsatisfied and alone because there was no spiritual dimension in his life, no connection with the eternal and no relationship with the Creator.

In reality, life is made that way. We were created by God and for God. We are not just citizens of the physical and material dimension; there is something within each of us that cries out for more than this. Jesus expressed this in his temptation experience: "Man shall not live by bread alone" (Matt 4:4 RSV). We have the image of God himself within us. Ecclesiastes writes that

God "has put eternity into man's mind" (Eccl 3:11 RSV). We are not made to be satisfied nor fulfilled by only the human dimension. And yet we persist in trying that and thus, sadly, we remain discontent. Augustine proclaimed it long ago: "Our heart is restless, until it rests in Thee." The writer Antoine De Saint-Exupery put it in modern terms:

> Ah, there is only one problem, only one in all the world. How can we restore to man a spiritual significance, a spiritual discontent; let something descend upon them like the dew of a Gregorian chant . . . don't you see, we cannot live any longer on refrigerators, politics, balance sheets and crossword puzzles. We simply cannot.

He is right—we cannot! Zacchaeus discovered this about his life, but he also discovered what to do about it. He went to see Jesus and found in him the answer to his emptiness and received a spiritual dimension, a vital connection with God and, therefore, life.

A famous actor was visiting with friends in a small town and his friends wanted their neighbors to meet the actor, so they had a party to introduce him to the people of the town. At the party, someone asked if the actor might perform for them. It was such a pleasant and eager group that he consented. He did some selections from Shakespeare and some parts from Broadway plays in which he had performed.

A retired minister, who was a close friend of the family, was there. Someone asked if there were something he would like to hear the actor do. He said there was, but he probably did not know it. The actor overheard and asked what it might be. The minister responded, "The Shepherd's Psalm, the Twenty-third Psalm." The actor said, "As a matter of fact, I do know it. I will do it, if after I finish, you will recite the Psalm for us too." The minister was reluctant, but the crowd was encouraging, so he agreed.

The actor began and it was beautifully done. His diction was perfect and his presentation was precise and eloquent. When he finished, the crowd applauded for several minutes. Then it was the minister's turn. He started hesitantly, but he got caught up in the depth and personal meaning the Psalm had for him. He remembered how throughout his ministry God had been there to shepherd and guide him. He remembered how just a few months before, he had journeyed through the valley of death in the loss of his dear wife and how God's presence had been his strength, comfort, and hope.

When he finished, there was total silence and tears were in many eyes. Then the veteran actor came over to the minister. He put his arm around the elderly pastor and said quietly, "You see, my friends, there is a difference here; I know the Shepherd's Psalm, but my friend here knows the Shepherd!"

To add life to our years, we need to know the Shepherd and have a spiritual dimension and a vital connection to the divine.

2. Second, to Add Life to Our Years We Need a Healthy Regard for Other People

It is vital to live a life that reaches out with love for others.

The most evident and outward result of Zacchaeus's experience with Jesus is that his life focus changes from himself to others. He is now concerned about his neighbors, his relationship with them, and their needs. Zacchaeus learned the hard way that looking out for number one was a self-defeating and lonely existence. He found that life was best experienced in reaching out to others.

David Woodyard, in his book *To Be Human Now*, has a chapter on the contemporary obscenities of life. He writes that the primary obscenities today are not pornography and foul language (bad as they are), but rather they are disengagement and dispassion. We make life obscene by our lack of involvement with one another and our simply not caring.

There was a *Peanuts* cartoon where Lucy decides that Linus, her little brother, needs to give up his security blanket. So while Linus is taking his afternoon nap, she slips his blanket away from him, takes it outside, and buries it in the ground. When Linus wakes up and realizes that his security blanket is gone, he goes into a mind-boggling panic attack. He can't breathe. He screams that he has to have that blanket, that he can't live without that blanket. Snoopy walks by and he sees Linus' big problem and Snoopy comes to the rescue! Snoopy rushes outside and with his trusty nose sniffs around until he finds the blanket. He digs up the blanket and dashes back to return it to a grateful Linus. With one hand Linus grabs the blanket and with his other arm he hugs Snoopy and thanks him excitedly, telling Snoopy that Snoopy has saved his life!

Linus is elated, and he and Snoopy celebrate and dance for joy over his reunion with his spiritual tourniquet, his blanket. In the final scene, Snoopy is lying on his doghouse thinking this thought: "Every now and then my existence is justified!"

When do you feel most alive, when do you feel that your existence is justified? Isn't it when you are doing something worthwhile for someone else? When you love others more than yourself?

There is an old story of two monks who are on their way back to their monastery when they are caught in a violent snowstorm. Struggling to make it back, they come across a man who has fallen and injured himself and is almost frozen to death. One of the monks tells the other that they must help get this man to the monastery or he will die in the elements. The other monk says that they cannot make it carrying the injured man and that they will all die. But the first insists that he will help the man, while the other decides to go on and save himself. The monk who stayed behind to help struggled and carried the man through the storm. Just before reaching the monastery, he tripped over a frozen body. It was the body of the monk who went on to save himself. The weather had overcome him, but the monk who helped the frozen man made it because his struggles and labor of carrying another had kept him from freezing. Jesus said, "Those who love their life lose it, and those who hate their life in this world will keep it for eternal life" (John 12:25).

Jesus was right, wasn't he? This is the way life works. We experience life best when we have a healthy relationship with God and a healthy regard for other people.

3. Third and Finally, to Add Life to Our Years, We Need a Healthy Reason to Hope

It is so important in life to have something to look forward to, something to hope for, and something to put your trust in.

Robert Frost describes those who missed real life in one of his poems: "Nothing to look backward to with pride, / And nothing to look forward to with hope." What more poignant description of the missed life can there be? But not so for Zacchaeus. His backward look was tainted, but because of Jesus he had something to look forward to each day now and even eternally.

We all need hope. We all need something to look forward to. We need the ability to move into the future without fear or dread, because if we lose hope in the future, our life in the present becomes powerless, empty, stagnant, and desolate. As Christians, we have hope because we have the promise of continual new beginnings, fresh starts. We believe in sanctifying grace and we live in the hope that God will continue to perfect us, grow us, and challenge us. The poet Louise Fletcher Tarkington expressed this desire and need: "I wish there were some wonderful place, / called the Land of Beginning Again."

Hope reminds us that there is this place and this power in the grace and love of God. And as Christians, we have the hope that nothing in life now and forever can defeat us. Hope is the buoyant spirit that raises us up when life knocks us down.

I miss *Calvin and Hobbes*, the great cartoon strip that was discontinued some time ago. In one of the episodes several years ago, Calvin comes marching into the living room early one morning. His mother is seated there in her favorite chair, sipping her morning coffee. She sees Calvin and is amused and amazed at how he is dressed. His head is encased in a large space helmet, a cape drapes around his neck, across his shoulders, and down his back, dragging on the floor, and in one hand he holds a flashlight and in the other a baseball bat. His mother asks him, "What's up today?" "Nothing so far," answers Calvin. "So far?" she questions. "Well, you never know," Calvin says, "Something could happen today." Then striding off, he proclaims, "And if anything does, I'm going to be ready for it!" His mom looks out to the reading audience and says, "I need a suit like that myself."

We have a suit like that—it's called hope. The Apostle Paul writing to the Christians in Rome expressed that hope powerfully: "Who shall separate us from the love of Christ? Shall tribulation, or distress, or persecution, or famine, or nakedness, or peril, or sword? . . . No, in all these things we are more than conquerors through him who loved us . . . [for nothing] in all creation . . . will be able to separate us from the love of God in Christ Jesus our Lord" (Rom 8:35, 37, 39 RSV).

When Paul Azinger, the pro golfer, was going through his battle with cancer, he was experiencing one of his darkest moments and was really feeling sorry for himself. His good friend, Johnny Miller, came to visit him. Paul shared with Johnny all that he thought he could accomplish and achieve if he could just get healthy again. Then he broke down and began to cry. Johnny Miller reached over and took hold of his hand and said, "You know, Zinger, what really counts in life is not what we accomplish or what we achieve, but rather what we overcome" (Paul Azinger and Ken Abraham, *Zinger: A Champion's Story of Determination, Courage, and Charging Back* [Grand Rapids: Zondervan, 1995], 234).

Hope in Christ promises us that we shall overcome. It is hope that gives up life even in the midst of life's most difficult circumstances. Also, as Christians, we have an eternal hope that our destiny is in God's hands.

A teenaged girl who had leukemia was visiting with her minister, who had come to see her in the hospital. She said to him, "I wish I didn't have leukemia, but really I'm not afraid. I know God is with me, and I know that we are on good terms." Can you say that? Are you and God on good terms right now? I hope so, because God is our hope. The poet John Greenleaf Whittier put it like this:

> I know not what the future hath
> Of marvel or surprise

Assured alone that life and death
His mercy underlies

We do not know what the future holds, but as Christians and followers of Christ, we do know Who holds our future.

Would you like to add life to your years? Jesus said, "I came that they may have life, and have it abundantly" (John 10:10).

Jesus came to offer life through faith, hope, and love, and you don't even have to climb a tree. It is a gift, you need only to accept it. So, a good prayer for us to pray today would be: "Lord, give me life and please give it to me right now."

CHAPTER FOUR

Lord, Give Me Hope

SCRIPTURE: PSALM 118:24

Have you ever heard of the utopian complex? It's a term used by psychologists and psychiatrists to describe people who go through life looking for the perfect situation and waiting for the perfect moment to do what they ought to do and to be what they ought to be. Meanwhile, life passes them by and they end up feeling frustrated and betrayed and empty and miserable. Let me illustrate this with a story.

In the early days of our country, a Native American princess went one morning to visit a neighboring tribe. The tribe she visited was known far and wide for their magnificent cornfields. The corn they produced each harvest was simply marvelous—without equal! No other tribe even came close. The princess asked if she might select one ear of corn from their field to take home and provide seed corn for her own tribe's fields the next year.

Graciously, her request was granted, but there was one condition. She would have to make her choice as she walked down the row! That is, she could not turn back and pick an ear of corn she had already passed by. So off she went, walking slowly down the row looking intently for that one perfect ear of corn. She walked and looked and pondered and studied, but she could not bring herself to pick an ear of corn for fear that there might just be a better one farther down the row.

All of a sudden she stepped out of the field and she realized what she had done. It hit her with a sickening thud! She had blown her opportunity! She had walked down the entire length of the row and still had not found that one absolutely perfect ear of corn. There was no turning back. Sadly, she had walked out of the field without making a choice, and so she went home empty-handed!

What a great parable this is for each one of us. Each day that we have is a gracious and generous gift from God. Each day provides us with many opportunities that will never come again. If you wait to select the perfect opportunity, you may miss the one opportunity that will benefit you the most. If you wait until that perfect date comes along, you may never go out. If you wait to join the one perfect cause in life, you may never contribute to anything. If you wait till you find the perfect job, you will be unemployed. If you delay participation in the spiritual life until things are just right, or until you think you are worthy, then you will miss out on life and faith and God. If you spend your life trapped in the utopian complex, looking for that perfect situation and waiting for that perfect moment to do what you know you ought to do, and to be what you know you ought to be, you may well discover too late that life has passed you by.

Like the Native American princess, you will have walked out of the cornfield frustrated—you will have ended up empty-handed.

Isn't this precisely what the psalmist was talking about many years ago? He put it like this: "This is the day that the LORD has made; let us rejoice and be glad in it!" In other words, don't wait around for another day! This is the only day we are sure of.

- Accept with gratitude this day!
- Embrace the joys of this day!
- Seize the opportunities of this day!
- Commit your life to God this day!

Now please don't misunderstand me. I am not singing the old hedonist song, "Eat, drink, and be merry, for tomorrow we may die." That's not what this is about. No! Rather, it's about seeing life in this world as a generous gift from God. It's about recognizing each day we have as a gracious gift from God and celebrating that, and seizing the precious opportunities it offers.

But the truth is that many people lose sight of that gift. Instead of "rejoicing in the day," they complain, whine, feel sorry for themselves, and are discontented with their lot in life. They never get around to "seizing the day" because they are waiting around for that perfect moment and looking for that perfect situation and dreaming of that perfect opportunity and longing for that perfect relationship and searching for that perfect job. It never happens for them because this is not a perfect world, and in this world there are no perfect situations.

Our hope as Christians is not wrapped up in this frazzled world and its imperfect circumstances. No! Our hope as Christians is wrapped up in God and his perfect love and grace. The hymn writer expressed it like this: "Our hope is built on nothing less / Than Jesus' blood and righteousness."

The people who refuse to learn this lesson will go through life waiting and looking for the perfect situation. It will not only be useless, but in most instances they will be miserable people. It's a basic truth of life: whatever is accomplished for good in this world is accomplished by the grace of God, using people who are imperfect and situations that are imperfect.

The good news of the Christian faith is this: God is perfect and he can, by the miracle of his love and grace, redeem and use imperfect people and imperfect circumstances. And that is our hope! Let me bring this closer to home and be more specific with three thoughts.

1. First, There Are No Perfect People

The sooner we learn this and accept this, the better off we will be. There was only one perfect person who has ever lived on the face of this earth, and his perfection threatened people so much that the world tried to destroy him. But even still, there are some people who are always looking for the perfect note, the perfect boss, the perfect neighbor, or the perfect friend. But then along comes the Christian faith to remind us that we don't just love people for what they are, but sometimes in spite of what they are. If we love people only when they please us, do what we want them to do, say what we want them to say, and look like we want them to look, then we are not really loving them at all. Rather, we are loving ourselves. We are loving the pleasure they bring us when they fit neatly into the mold we have designed.

D. L. Dykes spoke about this some years ago. He confessed that he used to give people what he called the Virtue Test. He would test them by a prize virtue and if they didn't measure up to that one particular virtue, he would write them off. Then Dr. Dykes said he realized one day how un-Christian that was. Here's how he put it:

> Many of us do it. We have a favorite virtue and we test everybody by it. And if anybody fails the test, we give up on them and mark them off our list. I had a hard time with this for a long time. I had certain virtues that I'd test people by. There was the drink test, the lie test, and the gossip test. If they didn't measure up to my test, then I had a hard time believing in them or working with them. The only trouble with this is what if that person knew everything about us? What if God did? And every time we failed to measure up in some area, He would cut us off . . . mark us off? Thank God . . . God doesn't work that way. As perfect as God is, God works with and through and for imperfect people. (Dr. D. L. Dykes, May 2, 1958).

Mary Ann Bird once wrote a short story that speaks to this. She entitled it "The Whisper Test." It is a true story from her own life. Mary Ann Bird said that she grew up knowing that she was different, and she hated that. She had some handicapping conditions that caused her young classmates at school to say things like "What happened to you?" Dealing with the questions and the stares were painful for her as a young child. She became convinced that no one outside of her family could ever love her.

When she reached second grade, Mary Ann Bird was put in Mrs. Leonard's room. Mrs. Leonard was the teacher who was adored by all the students. "She was short, round, happy—a sparkling lady."

Each year the students would be given a hearing test. Little Mary Ann dreaded the test because she was virtually deaf in one ear. However, she had discovered that if she did not press her hand as tightly on her ears as she had been instructed, she could pass the test. She knew from past years that the students would stand by the door and cover one ear, and the teacher, Mrs. Leonard, would sit at her desk a few feet away and whisper something, and the children would have to repeat it back. Things like, "The sky is blue" or "Do you have new shoes?"

Mary Ann Bird said, "I waited there for those words which God must have put into her mouth . . . those seven words that changed my life forever. In a beautiful whisper, Mrs. Leonard said, 'I wish you were my little girl' " (Rod Wilmoth, May 8, 1994).

When that happened—when that thoughtful, compassionate teacher did that, somewhere in heaven God was smiling, because that gesture was so Godlike. You see, God looks at all of us—and he sees our weaknesses and failures and foibles and inadequacies and handicaps and sins—and still he says, "I know you are not perfect, but I love you anyway and I want you to be My child!" God loves us not because we are good but because he is good; not because we are perfect but because he is; not because we are worthy, but because he is gracious. And God wants us to imitate his generous spirit in our dealings with other people. If you can't love other people for their sake, love them for God's sake! Let the love of God flow into you and out to others, because there are no perfect people.

2. Second, There Are No Perfect Marriages

If you see a marriage that looks perfect, you can be sure of one thing: they are working hard at it. Marriages may be made in heaven, but they have to be worked out on earth! Billy Graham was on *Oprah* some years ago. She asked him his secret of love, of being married to the same person for fifty-four years. Billy Graham said, "Ruth and I are happily incompatible!" Isn't that a great answer? It means they have learned how to love each other unconditionally.

Every couple is incompatible. You ask anybody who has lived with a married partner for even a few years, they will tell you that there are incompatibilities with every couple. But love means rising above those things —caring for one another in spite of those things. It means communication and negotiation and compromise and commitment and forgiveness and patience and understanding and kindness. It means giving the other person permission to be who they are—and not trying to force our way on them. It means unconditional love!

I was leading a marriage workshop some years ago. I asked this question: *How do you know your mate loves you?* One woman in the group gave an interesting answer. She said, "You're going to laugh when I tell you this, but I know my husband loves me because he gets me to the airport two hours before my scheduled flight." She was right. Everybody laughed, but she continued. "I know that sounds stupid, but I fly a lot in my business and I have this morbid fear that I'm going to miss my plane, and I want to get there two hours early. I know that's ridiculous and my husband knows it's ridiculous, but he does it. He gets me there because he knows it's important to me, and that's how I know he loves me!"

If you see what looks like a perfect marriage, you can know that a lot of that kind of sacrifice is going on in that relationship because real love knows that there are no perfect people and there are no perfect marriages.

3. Third and Finally,
There Are No Perfect Churches

Some people are always looking for the perfect church. They become "church tasters." They visit this church and then that church and then the other—and they taste and they test, they sample and they critique—but they never join. They search for the perfect church and wait for the perfect moment to join, but they do nothing. They never make a commitment to God and his church. They mean to do it, but they put it off and put it off to another day.

They remind me of the young man who thought he was in love with a certain girl, but he couldn't find just the right moment to ask her out. He decided to write her a love letter every day for a full year while waiting for that perfect moment to ask for a date. Three hundred sixty-five days and three hundred sixty-five love letters later, he went over to pop the question, only to discover that she had married the mailman!

If you are not in a church right now, get in one. If you are in the church, get into it a little deeper. Don't wait any longer. Don't put it off anymore. Commit your life as never before to God and his church. Just do it; do it now! Because this is the day the Lord has made; rejoice and be glad in it.

There may not be perfect situations in this life, but there is good news, and the good news is this: when we come to God in faith, God in his perfect grace can redeem and restore and save. Our hope is in God and his perfect love. So, because we are not perfect and because we need a lot of help and forgiveness and assurance from God, a good prayer that each one of us might pray personally today is this: "Lord, give me the hope that only comes from your amazing grace, and please give it to me right now."

CHAPTER FIVE

Lord, Give Me
Your Love

SCRIPTURE: JOHN 3:16

There are some scriptures that have become so familiar, so significant, so etched into our memories that the mere mention of their place in Scripture brings them to our mind and fills us with their power and meaning. For example, all I have to say is "The Twenty-third Psalm," and immediately, we think of God as our shepherd, who leads us into green pastures and beside still waters, and sees us through the valley of the shadow of death. Or when we hear 1 Corinthians 13, we think of the love chapter and the characteristics of love and those powerful closing words: "Faith, hope, and love abide . . . and the greatest of these is love." But perhaps the most memorable of all for us is John 3:16, which many have called the gospel in summary, the gospel in a nutshell: "God so loved the world that he gave his only Son so that everyone who believes in him may not perish but may have eternal life."

Sometimes with something that is so familiar to us, if we are not careful we can miss the power and the meaning. So to help us understand the depth of God's love, I want you to use your imagination and make two lists: (1) Those you would die for. (2) Those you would sacrifice your son, daughter, grandson, granddaughter, nephew, or niece for. Did anyone make your second list? No one made mine! But that's exactly what God did. God gave his Son, and you and I made the list. That's the kind of love God has for us. God's love is unconditional and incomprehensible. Let me suggest a description that may help us understand the depth of this love and put it into perspective. God's love is the kind of love that will not let us go, that will not let us down, and that will not let us off. Let's take a look at each of these.

1. First of All, God's Love Will Not Let Us Go

One of the major themes of the Bible is what we call the divine initiative. Life and salvation begin with God, not us. This means that God reaches out to us and seeks us out in love and grace.

The concept of the seeking God is unique to the Judeo-Christian faith. It is not found in any other religion or faith. From the beginning to the end, the Bible is the story of the God who seeks his people and despite their unresponsiveness and unfaithfulness, does not give up on them. God will not let them go. God pursued Israel and pursues us with the indestructible love of a parent. In the closing of the Twenty-third Psalm, the phrase "Surely goodness and mercy shall follow me all the days of my life" can also be correctly translated, "Surely goodness and mercy shall pursue me all the days of my life." God with his goodness and mercy does not trail along behind us, but rather he pursues us and chases us down.

The psalmist also wrote: "Whither shall I go from thy spirit? or whither shall I flee from thy presence? If I ascend up into heaven, thou art there: if I make my bed in hell, behold, thou art there" (Psalm 139:7-8 KJV). The hymn writer describes God as the "love that will not let me go."

In Luke 15, Jesus described God as a seeking shepherd, a searching woman, and a waiting father. Francis Thompson, in his poem describing his experience with God, called God "The Hound of Heaven." God does not give up on us even if everyone else does and even if we give up on ourselves. God's love will not let us go!

2. Second, God's Love Will Not Let Us Down

The second great theme in the Bible is the dependability of God's love. You can count on it. You can bet your very life on it. This great characteristic of God is described in the Old Testament by the Hebrew word *hesed*. It is one of the primary words in the Old Testament used to describe God, and this fascinating word is a forerunner of the New Testament's *agape* and *grace*. *Hesed* is translated primarily as "steadfast love." It also has connotations of mercy and kindness, but it essentially means God's amazing faithfulness and love. It means that God keeps his promises. It means that we can trust and depend on God and his love. God's love will not let us down. Even in a world of mistrust and broken trust, even when we are unfaithful and undependable, God is dependable and trustworthy. Paul says in Romans that nothing "in all creation . . . will be able to separate us from the love of God in Christ Jesus our Lord" (8:39).

In 1989 an earthquake hit Armenia and killed over 30,000 people. One of the areas that was hit especially hard by the earthquake contained an elementary school. After the tremors had ceased, a father of one of the students raced to the school to see about his son. When he arrived on the scene, he was stunned to find that the building had been leveled. Looking at the mass of stones and rubble, he remembered a promise he had made to his little boy. He had told him, "No matter what happens, I'll always be there for you." Remembering his promise, he found the area closest to his son's room and began to pull back the rocks. Others had also come and said to him, "It's too late! You know they are dead; you can't help." Even a policeman urged him to give up. But he refused. For eight hours, then sixteen, then thirty-two, then thirty-six he continued to dig through the rubble. His hands were raw and his energy was gone, but he refused to quit. Finally, after thirty-eight wrenching hours, he pulled back a boulder and heard voices and recognized his son's among them. He called his boy's name, "Arman! Arman!" A voice answered him, "Dad, it's me!" Then the boy said, "I told the other kids not to worry. I told them if you were alive, you'd save me, and when you saved me they'd be saved too. Because you promised, 'No matter what, I'll always be there for you.' I knew you would never give up or let me down" (Jack Canfield and Mark Victor Hansen, *Chicken Soup for the Soul* [Deerfield Beach, Fla.: Heath Communications, 1993], 273-74).

We never know when life is going to blindside us. Sometimes circumstances in life make us feel as if we have been hit by an emotional earthquake and have been buried beneath a rubble of distress, hurt, and disappointment. We feel helpless, hopeless, and alone, but we are not. For God will not let us down. God has not forgotten his greatest promise: "I will be with you." And his presence is power and hope. God's love will not let us down.

Perhaps Jesus put it best in John 16:33: "In the world you have tribulation" (that means trial, trouble, distress, problems, crisis, betrayal, and so forth) "but be of good cheer" (which means take courage, have faith, be brave), for "I have overcome the world" (RSV). And "Lo, I am with you alway, even unto the end of the world" (Matt 28:20 KJV). God's love will not let us down.

One popular book that illustrates God's love is *The Shack*. It is the story of a man who in the midst of an extreme tragedy meets God face-to-face. The main theme of this moving book is that God is good. Regardless of the circumstances and tragedies of our life, we must believe and trust that God is good and that God will be with us with strength and help. A colleague of mine has recently lived this out in her life. After a courageous battle with cancer, her daughter died. Throughout this walk through the valley of death with her daughter, she held on to her faith and God held on to her. She lived and held on using a special mantra, which she said to herself every day: "God is good; cancer stinks, God is with us." God's love did not let her down. It carried her through and carries her now in her grief. God's love will not let us down; we can count on it.

3. Third and Finally, God Will Not Let Us Off

God's love holds us accountable for the gifts, talents, and grace we have received. The Bible always holds grace and accountability in balance. We often do not. We are like the woman who wanted her husband's two favorite songs to be played at his funeral. They were "Amazing Grace" and "I Did It My Way." Often we are like that man. We want God's amazing grace, but we want to be in control and do it our way. But we can't have it that way. God's love won't let us go and won't let us down, but it also will not let us off.

We are saved to serve. We are loved to love. We are blessed to be a blessing. Love calls for commitment, for self-sacrifice, for the giving of ourselves. In the parable of the Prodigal Son, we must not forget that the father lets the prodigal in again, but does not let him off; he is given the family ring and is responsible to live as a son of the father, with duties and responsibilities. God accepts us as we are but seeks to make us what we can be.

When I was growing up, my brother and I were extremely competitive with each other. We could make a competition out of anything: who could eat the fastest, who could go to sleep first, and so forth. One day, leaving the community park, we decided to race home and see who could get in the house first. We arrived at the front door at the same time, and in our pushing and shoving we tore off the screen door. As you might expect, it upset our father. But he was not so upset about the door; he could fix it easily. Our dad could fix anything. He was upset with our competitiveness and our fighting. He loved us and wanted us to love each other. It hurt him when we competed and fought. He wanted us to be our best. He would not let us off. He wanted us to be loving brothers.

God too must be hurt and disappointed as he looks down on our world and our lives and sees how competitive we are with one another. God sees our world fighting and at war, and that is not what pleases him. He wants us to live in harmony, peace, and love.

Like that of a good father, God's love is unconditional, but it calls for our best. We are to love God with all that we are, but we also are to love our neighbors as ourselves and minister to the least of our brothers and sisters. God's love will not let us off.

E. V. Hill was a longtime pastor of a large African American congregation in the Watts area of Los Angeles and a friend of Billy Graham. During the burnings, lootings, and community riots that rocked the Watts area in the 1960s, Dr. Hill spoke out against this kind of violence and protest. He chastised those in his community who destroyed property and stole from the area's merchants.

Hill's stance and outspoken sermons brought threats to him and his church. As the tension and threats grew in the community, one evening he received a phone call at his home. His wife noticed how serious and solemn he became during and after the call. She asked him about it, but he said, "It was nothing." She knew better and pressed him to tell her what it was all about. "It was a threat, wasn't it?" she asked. Finally, he told her. He said, "They have threatened to blow up our car with me in it." They held each other and cried; they knew that there was no way that they could guard their car and protect it 24 hours a day. That night they went to bed and held each other until finally they fell asleep.

The next morning, when Dr. Hill awoke, he noticed that his wife was not in bed, she was already up. That was not unusual, but when he went into the kitchen, she was not there, nor anywhere else in the house. He began to become alarmed, and even more so when he noticed that the car was gone from the carport. But before he could call the police, his wife came walking in the back door.

"Where have you been?" he asked. She said, "I drove the car around the block to make sure it would be safe for you to drive to work this morning." When Dr. Hill tells this story, he says, "I never have to wonder or ask if my wife loves me." He had seen her love in action.

We need not wonder about God's love for us. We have seen it in action. We need only look to Jesus, we need only look at the cross and know that God so loved the world that he gave his only son. That's God's love: a love that will not let us go, will not let us down, and will not let us off. Thanks be to God for his marvelous love!

So, a good prayer for us to pray today is "Lord, give me your love and please give it to me right now."

CHAPTER SIX

Lord, Give Me Grace

SCRIPTURE: EPHESIANS 2:4-10

Some years ago, Jay Leno was doing his "Man on the Street" interviews and he asked some college students questions to measure their knowledge about the Bible. "Can you name one of the Ten Commandments?" he asked. One student replied, "Freedom of speech?" Then Jay asked another student, "Can you complete this sentence? *Let that one who is without sin . . .*" Her response was, "Have a good time?" Jay then turned to a young man and asked, "Who, according to the Bible, was swallowed by a whale?" The young man smiled with confidence and said, "Oh, I know that one —Pinocchio!"

That interview reminded me of the question a minister asked a friend one day: "What do you think of when I say the word *grace?*" To which his friend replied, "Why, Grace is a blue-eyed blond." Some years ago, Dr. R. Lofton Hudson wrote a book with a similar title. He called it *Grace Is Not a Blue-eyed Blonde* (Waco, Texas: Word Books, 1968).

It is amazing how little we know about the religious and theological terms we use so often. Most of us would not respond to a question about the definition of grace as being a blue-eyed blond, but we might be hard-pressed to give an adequate and relevant answer. The grace of God is at the heart of the New Testament; it is the basis of our faith; it is the core of United Methodist theology. Let me share with you a working definition of grace in the hope that this will give us a better understanding of what grace is really all about and why it really is "amazing!"

Without question, grace is at the core of the Christian faith. The word *grace* is one of the most profound words in the New Testament. It is full of meaning and message. Interestingly, the New Testament does not define grace, but rather simply points to Jesus as the embodiment and demonstration of God's grace in our world. The Gospel of John proclaims: "The Word became flesh and dwelt among us, full of grace and truth" (1:14 RSV). One preacher called grace the shorthand word for the whole gospel. It captures the essence of God's attitude and relationship with us.

The word translated *grace* in the Greek is *charis*, from which we get the word *charity*, but it literally means "favor." Grace is the unmerited, unearned, and undeserved favor of God. The gospel message is that God gives his grace through Jesus Christ to persons of every age, time, and station, who have done nothing to deserve it. It is a gift and can only be accepted. One person put it this way: "Mercy is not getting what you deserve. But grace is getting what you don't deserve."

The comics sometimes have a way of expressing great and deep thoughts through the use of humor. For example, I discovered an interesting insight into grace in one of the *Dennis the Menace* cartoons. As you are aware, Dennis is indeed a menace and pest to his neighbors, Mr. and Mrs. Wilson. Yet Mrs. Wilson continues to be kind and gracious to Dennis. In this particular cartoon, Dennis and his little friend Joey are leaving Mrs. Wilson's house with their hands full of cookies, and Joey says, "I wonder what we did to deserve this?" Dennis answers with great insight: "Look, Joey, Mrs. Wilson gives us cookies not because we're nice, but because she's nice."

God loves us and seeks us not because we are lovable but because God is love. And that's grace!

John Wesley saw all of life lived in the context of grace. He explained it in terms of the stages of grace in which we live. First, we experience *prevenient grace*. This grace seeks us before we know it, gives us the ability to have faith, creates within us a spiritual discontent. Prevenient grace prepares, prompts, and prods us until we experience the *saving grace* of God. Then saving grace forgives us, gives us a fresh start, turns us in the right direction, and gives us an eternal destiny. And finally, Wesley speaks of *sanctifying grace*, that grace in which we live the rest of our lives. The grace that seeks to make us both whole and holy. Wesley challenged us to always be growing in grace.

Wesley's stages of grace only tell us about the where and when of grace. Now I will define and illustrate the *what* of grace. Grace is God's forgiving love, God's accepting love, and God's empowering love. It cannot be earned; it is a gift, not an award or reward for anything we have done. It arises out of God's goodness and mercy and is revealed and shared in Jesus Christ, our Lord and Savior. Let's look together at these three thoughts.

1. First of All, Grace Is First and Foremost God's Forgiving Love

We have broken and distorted our relationship with God, we have gone our own way, we have journeyed into the far country and squandered our gifts and life, we have rebelled against God's authority over us, and we have ignored his love and care. Paul said "all have sinned and fall short of the glory of God" (Rom 3:23).

However we put it, we stand in need of God's forgiveness to restore us to a vital and growing relationship with God, our Creator. And when we need forgiveness, human or divine, there is nothing we can do except ask for that forgiveness. But God, in Jesus, has already offered us forgiveness and restoration, even before we ask for it. God's grace takes the initiative and in Jesus we are forgiven. Grace is God's forgiving love. A gift from God to you.

There is a wonderful story of forgiveness about William and Catherine Booth, who were the founders of the Salvation Army. There was a young man named Alexander who had become active in the Salvation Army. William and Catherine had taken to the young man and liked him so well that he seemed almost like a son to them. He seemed so capable and trustworthy that they made him their financial officer to look after their funds. For a while, everything went along wonderfully and Alexander did a really fine job. But then one day it came to light that Alexander was actually embezzling funds from them, and huge sums at that. So he was arrested, convicted, and sentenced to prison.

But the first day he was permitted to receive mail, there was a letter to him from William Booth. The first day Alexander was permitted to have visitors, two people were there to see him, William and Catherine Booth. And every visitor's day, Alexander could count on two people being there to see him: William and Catherine Booth, the very people he had betrayed and hurt. When his prison term was finally over, he walked out of the prison, and they were there to meet him.

Catherine said to him, "Alexander, this is a great day! You're free, so let's go celebrate." She had packed a picnic lunch, and the three of them went over to a little park and had a picnic together. And when they were finishing, a really special thing happened. William looked at Alexander and said, "Son, Mrs. Booth and I have been doing a lot of talking and praying, and we have something we'd like to ask you to do." Alexander looked at him with a very surprised and startled expression as if to say, "What in the world could it be?" And then William reached into the picnic basket and pulled out a money bag and handed it to Alexander. "Son," he said, "Mrs. Booth and I would like for you to come back to work for us. We'd like for you to be our bookkeeper and our treasurer once again." That's grace, forgiving love!

William and Catherine Booth knew about grace, for they had experienced God's grace—God's forgiving love—and that day they shared it with Alexander. That's the kind of love, forgiving love, that God has for each of us.

2. Second, Grace Is Also God's Accepting Love

Reuel Howe says we have three needs in life: love, acceptance, and discipline, and we need them on a divine and perfect level. Grace is accepting love. It is God's love that accepts us as we are. It is what one writer calls "in spite of love"; that is, God loves us even in spite of our weaknesses, foibles, and failures. We know a lot about "because of love," but we know far too little about this "in spite of love." God's grace is love that cares for us in spite of what we are or what we have done, or what we become or fail to become. This does not mean that God isn't often disappointed in us and brokenhearted over our misuse of life and others. This is because he loves us and wants the best for us.

My father died when my brother and I were in our early teens and our sister was six years old. I still remember the last time my father disciplined me. In those days, that meant a spanking in the woodshed. And I remember the reason I was spanked. It was because my brother and I had gotten into a fight that day. Both of us got our spankings, but what was worse than the physical pain was the pain that we brought to our father's heart. As I mentioned in chapter 5, it hurt him and disappointed him that his boys were fighting with each other. He loved us and accepted us as his boys, but he did not approve of our competition and fighting. God too accepts us and loves us even when he does not approve of our attitude and our behavior. God's grace is accepting love, and he accepts us just as we are.

A minister tells about his experience at a three-day retreat in the Midwest. On the retreat, he kept hearing from participants about a church member who had touched their lives by the contagion of her witness and the reality of her love. He learned that this person was now dying of cancer. She came to the retreat a little late and had a great bandage over half of her face because the disease had caused the loss of an eye and part of her face. The minister finally got the opportunity to meet her and talk with her. He shared with her about the many whose lives had been touched and blessed by her love and prayers. In their brief meeting they became bonded to one another. As they were about to leave, she took him aside and asked a favor. She said, "May I show you what I look like under this bandage?" He said, "I think so." Off in a corner, alone, she took off her bandage, and there was just nothing there. After about fifteen seconds, she put her bandage back on, and she hugged him and said, "Thank you. I needed somebody to see me as I am and love me anyway." That's grace!

God sees and accepts us as we are—warts and wounds and scars and all—and loves us still!

3. Finally, Grace Is God's Empowering Love

The third element of grace is often left out, but I feel that it is an essential ingredient to understanding grace. Grace is empowering love, love that changes us, gives us new direction, motivates us, sustains us, helps us, strengthens us. We do need the power of God's love in our lives, don't we?

It is one thing to know that we need to change; it is another to have the power to change. God's grace is that power. John writes in his Gospel: "To all who received him, who believed in his name, he gave power to become children of God" (John 1:12).

A minister friend of mine tells about a call he received from a family in his church. They were concerned about their teenage daughter. She had recently broken up with her boyfriend, and she was very depressed. She was not eating properly, was crying a lot, and was just staying in her room avoiding everyone. They wanted my minister friend to come by and talk to her. He agreed and arrived at their home just before school let out, so he would be there when she got home.

He was sitting at the kitchen table with her mom drinking a cup of coffee. Her little brother was there at the table also, having his after-school snack. Suddenly, they heard the door open and heard the daughter come in. Amazingly, she was singing, there was a smile on her face, and she greeted them warmly as she passed through! No signs of sadness at all. She seemed on top of the world. They looked at each other, confused. But then the little brother quickly analyzed the situation and summed it all up perfectly. He said, "She's got a new boyfriend; ain't love grand?"

Love is grand, but it is more than grand. Love is life changing! Love has the power to change us and to enable us to discover life in all its abundance. God's love is empowering love, empowering us to change and empowering us to stand against the storms of life.

Grace is not a blue-eyed blonde, but it is for blondes, brunettes, and redheads; God's grace is for all of us. As the poet John Newton put it:

Amazing grace! How sweet the sound
That saved a wretch like me!
I once was lost, but now I am found;
Was blind, but now I see.

God's grace is forgiving love, accepting love, empowering love. It is a gift from God to you and me, but it only works if we receive it. So, our prayer for this day might well be: Lord, please give me grace and give it to me right now!

CHAPTER SEVEN

Lord, Give Me a Resurrection

SCRIPTURE: JOHN 11:38-44 AND LUKE 24:1-5

From the very beginning, we in the church have loved to sing our faith. And with good reason: we have a faith worth singing about!

I don't know about you, but I love all the different kinds and varieties of faith music. I love the majestic anthems of Bach and the gospel songs of Fannie Crosby. I love the exuberant music of Mozart and the powerful hymns of Charles Wesley. I love Handel's *Messiah* and Newton's "Amazing Grace." I love camp songs and folk songs and French carols. However, for me, some of the most moving and powerful expressions of faith music are found in those great and poignant spirituals that come out of African American culture.

Often written in painful and debilitating circumstances, the spirituals cover the full range of human emotions—joy and sorrow, confidence and despair, praise and lament, victory and defeat—but always there is that dominant and recurring theme of eternal hope. Things may be hard now, times may be tough now, but ultimately God will win, and if we remain faithful, he will share his victory with us. All through the great spirituals we hear it: the resurrection theme—death is not death at all. It's victory; it is going home to be with God.

In the spirituals, we hear a number of crucial ideas repeated dramatically. For example, we hear the good news of Jesus Christ proclaimed and celebrated like this:

Go, tell it on the mountain,
Over the hills and everywhere,
Go, tell it on the mountain
That Jesus Christ is born.

And we hear the challenge of discipleship:

This little light of mine,
I'm goin' to let it shine.
Let it shine, let it shine, let it shine.

I'm gonna sing when the Spirit says a sing,
I'm gonna shout when the Spirit says a shout,
I'm gonna pray when the Spirit says a pray,
And obey the Spirit of the Lord.

We find also in the spirituals a strong reliance on the comforting presence of Christ in times of trouble:

Nobody knows the trouble I see, Lord!
Nobody knows like Jesus.

I want Jesus to walk with me . . .
In my trials . . .
When I'm in trouble . . .
When my heart is almost breaking . . .
And when my head is bowed in sorrow . . .
I want Jesus to walk with me.

But most of all in these amazing spirituals, we find the hope of resurrection, the strong belief that death is victory—that death is not death at all; it's going home to be with God. Look at these words:

Soon I will be done with the troubles of the world . . .
I'm goin' home to live with God

In that great gettin' up morning,
Fare ye well . . . fare ye well.

Swing low, sweet chariot,
Coming for to carry me home.

Over and over in these African American spirituals, we hear this powerful theme of resurrection. Death is not the end but the beginning. Death is nothing to be afraid of. It is merely a door through which we pass to move into a deeper and more meaningful relationship with God. For the people of faith, death is a victorious homegoing! It's going home to be with God.

This is the good news of Easter, isn't it? But you know, we don't have to wait till we die. Eternal life can begin for you and me now. Resurrection can happen for you and me now. New life is available for you and me right now. We don't have to wait till we physically die to be at home with God.

Now, please don't misunderstand me. I believe in that "Great Gettin' Up Morning" off in the future, but I also believe that God can raise us up now—that God has a power to bring us out of those dark and dismal tombs that imprison us and enslave us and smother the very life out of us. Do you feel trapped? Do you feel imprisoned, paralyzed, shackled, buried by some problem? Do you feel locked up in some spiritual grave? Is there something in your life right now that is smothering you to death, sapping your strength, depleting your energy, destroying your soul? Is it some weakness? Is it an addiction? Is it emptiness within? Is it some remorse over some wrong that you have done? Or something you've failed to do? Is it guilt? Or shame? Or vengeance? Is it some heavy burden, or some secret sin, or some sorrow that's covering you over like a heavy blanket? Do you feel trapped in some desolate and dreary tomb?

If so, I have good news. God has a resurrection for you! He wants to bring you out into the light again. He wants to bring you out of that tomb and give you a new start. And listen! He has the power to do it. He can bring you back to life.

This powerful story in John 11 speaks to this. Remember it with me. Mary and Martha, who live in Bethany, are some of Jesus' closest friends. They send word to him that their brother, whose name is Lazarus, is desperately ill. "Please come. We need your help. Hurry. He is sinking fast." But by the time Jesus gets there, Lazarus has died and has been in his grave for four days. Mary and Martha come out to meet Jesus, and they express their grief: "He's gone. We've lost him. O Lord, if only you had been here, our brother would not have died."

The family and friends have gathered and in their deep sorrow, they begin to weep over the loss of their loved one, Lazarus. The heart of Jesus goes out to them, and Jesus weeps with them. He loves Lazarus too. He loves them and shares their pain. Jesus goes out to the cavelike tomb, and he says to them: "Roll back the stone!" Martha, always the realist and ever ready to speak out, protests: "But Lord, we can't do that. He has been in the grave for four days. By now there will be a terrible odor." Jesus says to her: "Martha, only believe and you will see the power of God."

So they roll the stone away, and Jesus cries out in a loud voice: "Lazarus, come out!" And incredibly, miraculously, amazingly, before their very eyes—Lazarus is resurrected! He comes out of the tomb. He still has on his grave clothes. His head and feet are still wrapped with mummylike bandages. Jesus then turns to the friends and family and says to them, "Unbind him and let him go. Unwrap him and set him free."

In this graphic and dramatic story are three awesome lessons. Three great truths emerge that can be helpful to us today. Let me list them for us: Jesus wept with those he loved and he still does. Jesus raised people up and he still does. Jesus included others in the healing process, and he still does.

1. First, Jesus Wept with Those He Loved, and He Still Does

John 11:35 is the shortest verse in the Bible: *Jesus wept* (KJV). That verse served me well when I was a little boy in Sunday school. Back then if you could quote a verse of Scripture, you would get a gold star by your name on the big chart on the wall. This was my star-producing verse! "Anybody know a verse of Scripture this morning?" the teacher would say, and my hand would go up immediately. "John 11:35 . . . Jesus wept."

The next Sunday the same thing would happen. "Anybody ready to quote a verse of Scripture?" Up with the hand. "John 11:35 . . . Jesus wept." Another gold star. After several Sundays of this, the teacher finally looked at me and said, "Jim, do you know any verse other than John 11:35, Jesus wept?"

A few years ago, a young ministerial student was working at our church as a summer intern. He went over to the chapel one Sunday morning to serve Holy Communion. He had never served communion alone before, and he was scared. Back then we had a communion ritual printed on a laminated card. It started with the Invitation to Communion, followed by the Prayer of Confession and the Prayer of Consecration; and then just before the people would come forward to receive communion, the minister would stand, face the congregation, and say, "Hear these words of comfort from the Scriptures." We left a blank there on the communion card so the minister in charge could at that point quote a favorite verse. When they got to this point in the service, the young ministerial student stood and said, "Hear these words of comfort from the Scriptures . . ." And then he went absolutely blank. There was a long pause, and then he blurted out the only verse he could think of at the moment: "Jesus wept."

Later he told me what happened and how awful he felt about that at first, but then how one of our members came down after the service and said to him, "When you quoted that verse, 'Jesus wept,' that was so meaningful to me because it made me suddenly realize that the Healer of our pain is the feeler of our pain!"

There is a minister serving now in one of our eastern states named Ed. Ed tells a powerful story about his early days in the ministry. Ed says he came out of seminary ready to be "super preacher." Single-handedly he would solve all the problems of the world. He had been trained, he was well prepared, and now as a pastor in a little community in his home state, he was ready to be "super preacher." He had all the answers, and he was ready to spout them to the world with pious religious authority. And that he did as the months passed quickly into years.

Then one morning the phone rang. The father of his board chairman had suddenly died. As Ed started to their home, it hit him: "I don't know what to do. I'm their pastor, and I'm scared. I don't know what to say to them." He tried to remember his classes in pastoral care. He tried to recall appropriate Scripture passages to quote. He tried to think of some profound theological message to give these people in their shocked hour of need. He plotted his strategy: "I know what I'll do. I'll go in boldly and take charge. I'll gather all the family in the living room and quote the Twenty-third Psalm. That's what I'll do," said Ed. "That's the answer."

But there was one thing Ed hadn't counted on. When he got to the home and gathered the family in the living room, he looked at their faces and their pain became his pain. He suddenly realized how much he loved these wonderful people, and his heart broke with them. He was overcome with emotion. As he tried to quote the Twenty-third Psalm, he said, "The Lord is my Shepherd," and then Ed exploded into tears. He cried so hard that the family had to rush over and minister to him. They helped him over to the couch, mopped his brow with a cold cloth, and brought him a glass of water. Ed was so embarrassed, so ashamed. He felt that he had failed miserably. He was humiliated. He got through the funeral and went immediately to the bishop and asked to be moved to another church. And shortly after, Ed was indeed transferred.

Several years passed and each year at annual conference, Ed would hide from that family. He could not face them. But then one evening he came around a corner and there they were. He couldn't avoid them. He couldn't hide. Their faces lit up when they saw Ed. They ran to him and hugged him warmly. "Oh, Ed," they said, "we are so glad to see you. Our family loves you. We appreciate you so much. We miss you. We talk about you all the time. We have loved all of our pastors, but you are the one who helped us the most." "Oh, really?" Ed said with genuine surprise. "Oh, yes," they said, "We'll never forget how you came and cried with us when Daddy died!"

There's an important lesson here. When people are in grief, they don't want theological pronouncements. They just want us to come and love them. They just want us to come and cry with them.

Jesus wept with those he loved—and he still does. He hurts with us. He feels our pain. We all face suffering some time, and when it comes, one thing we can know is that our Lord is hurting with us. He will love us through it. Jesus will walk through the valley with us, and in time he will bring us out of the valley of sorrow to the mountaintop on the other side. Jesus wept with those he loved, and he still does.

2. Second, Jesus Raised People Up, and He Still Does

The noted minister Dr. D. L. Dykes said that when he was a student pastor just starting out in the ministry, he really wanted to learn how to do things right. So each time he was called on to do something new, he would go to the Bible and find out how Jesus performed that ministerial task and learn from him.

All went well until he was called on to do his first funeral. He turned to the New Testament only to discover that Jesus performed no funerals, only resurrections! Here in John 11, Jesus resurrects Lazarus. He raises him up and brings him out of the tomb. "Lazarus, come forth," he says.

See how personal this is! Jesus calls him by name. If you will listen carefully, you can hear him calling your name. He has a resurrection for you. He wants to bring you out of that tomb (whatever it is) that is imprisoning you. He wants to set you free. And he has the power to do it. If you will hear his call and respond in faith, he will raise you up and give you a new start, a new chance, a new life.

Jesus wept with those he loved, and he still does. Jesus raised people up, and he still does.

3. Third and Finally, He Included Other People in the Healing Process, and He Still Does

Don't miss this now. Notice what happens when Lazarus comes out of the tomb. Jesus turns to his family and friends and says, "Unbind him and let him go. Unwrap him and set him free."

It's amazing to me that some people think the small group movement is a new thing. Small groups, support groups, are as old as the Bible, and they are so essential. Jesus knew how important it is to have our family and our friends helping us, surrounding us with love, supporting us, encouraging us, setting us free in every moment, but especially in those dramatic moments when we are trying to make a new start with our lives.

Recently a man stopped by to see me. A little over a year ago, he went through a great personal tragedy. He is coming through it with the help of God and with the help of the church, especially his Sunday school class. He said, "I was devastated. I was disillusioned and defeated and saw no hope for the future and no relief for my pain. I was so hurt that I was immobilized. All the life had drained out of me, but God brought me back to life . . . and this church has been there for me every step of the way. My Sunday school class has been so incredible. I don't know what I would have done without them. I couldn't have made it without them."

You know what he was saying, don't you? He was saying, "God brought me out of the tomb, and my friends helped me, and supported me . . . and together, by the grace of God, they loved me back to life."

Jesus wept with those he loved, and he still does. He raised people up, and he still does. He included others in the healing process, and he still does. This is the good news of Easter. It is the good news of the Christian faith: Christ is risen, and he can resurrect us! So, this is a good prayer that we can pray today: "Lord, give me a resurrection and please, God, give it to me right now."

CHAPTER EIGHT

Lord, Give Me
Your Spirit

SCRIPTURE: ACTS 1:6-8; 2:1-6

Before ascending to the Father, the Risen Christ promised his disciples that he would be with them always through the gift of the Holy Spirit. He promised that they would receive power when the Spirit came upon them, and he charged them to be his witnesses beginning in Jerusalem, Judea, and Samaria and out to the ends of the earth. And on the day of Pentecost it happened! It was a sudden powerful and dramatic event that defied description. They could only say it was like the sound of a mighty, rushing wind, and there was the appearance of tongues of fire and harmonious, understandable, and incredible communication. The Spirit of God had come upon them and they had become the church of Jesus Christ. They and the world would never be the same again! They had received the gift of the Holy Spirit, and with that gift they had received four things that they desperately needed, and indeed four things we all need:

- The Gift of Presence
- The Gift of Pulse
- The Gift of Purpose
- The Gift of Power

1. The Gift of the Spirit Was First and Foremost a Gift of Presence

Jesus had tried to prepare the disciples for his death, resurrection, and ascension; to get them ready for the time in which he would no longer be with them in person. He promised that the Spirit would come to them and that they would not be comfortless and alone. The very Spirit of God that was within Jesus would be with them even until the end of time.

John Wesley's experience at Aldersgate when he felt his heart strangely warmed was an experience of the presence of God and that sense of presence and its assurance became central to his preaching and the Methodist movement in England and America. In a time when people felt that God was far away, unknown and unknowable, Wesley proclaimed the nearness and availability of a God who through the Spirit was nearer than breathing and closer than hands and feet.

The message for us today is that God is with us and that his presence is daily, not occasional. In the book *Children's Letters to God*, a little girl expressed it well when she wrote to God: "Dear God: I don't ever feel alone anymore, since I found out about you, Love, Nora." This is the good news of the Christian faith: we are not alone; the very presence of God is with us.

John Killinger tells of a young boy and his grandfather who are out fishing from a dock. As they fish together, they begin to philosophize about why sunsets are red and who makes the rain fall and why the seasons change and other secrets of the universe. Finally, the boy asks his grandfather: "Does anyone ever see God?" The grandfather answers: "It's getting so I hardly see anything else."

The Christian faith calls us to that kind of awareness and vision. How many times have we felt it: "Surely the presence of the Lord is in this place!" It is the amazing gift of God's presence.

2. Second, the Gift of the Spirit Is Also a Gift of Pulse, a Gift of Life

Following the death of Jesus, the disciples were emotional wrecks filled with apprehension, fear, and hopelessness. The resurrection overcame some of their fears and filled them with hope, but they were still stunned and confused. Christ had risen from the dead and they had experienced the Risen Lord on a number of occasions, but they were still unsure of where they would go from here. What in the world could they do without him?

Jesus told them to wait and the Spirit would come upon them. On the day of Pentecost it happened, and they got resurrected too! They became the church of Jesus Christ. The church became alive.

It is interesting to note that the word for "spirit" in the Old Testament is *ruach*, which also means "the wind." The word for spirit in the New Testament is *pneuma*, which means "breath" or "air." The spirit came like the wind and breathed life into the disciples and into the church. It was like the disciples had received CPR. They were revived and renewed with spirit, breath, new energy—and new life!

It was like a reenactment of Ezekiel's vision and experience in the valley of dry bones. When the Spirit came upon those dry bones, the bones came together and found new life! That is precisely what happened to those early disciples. The wind of the Holy Spirit blew upon them, and they came alive!

There is a story told of a young man who served his country during the Vietnam War. He was the lead man on a jungle patrol; he was the person responsible for looking for land mines, booby traps, and ambushes. With every step he risked death, and if he made a mistake, his entire unit would be in danger. When the war was finally over, he couldn't believe that he was still alive while so many of his friends had not survived. He often felt that he would have been better off if he had died. He was haunted constantly by nightmares of his friends dying. Slowly his spirit was robbed of life. He saw many doctors and had many tests, but no one had a cure for his myriad ills. He continued to decline as time passed.

One day he visited the Vietnam Memorial in Washington, D.C. Tears flowed freely as he touched the names of friends etched in the hard black stone. He looked for and found every name he remembered except one. Back and forth he walked, touching the wall, looking for the one last name. He looked in the book that listed all the names and told where to find them on the wall. He asked the attendant, but the attendant could not find the name either.

"Are you sure that's the right name?" the attendant asked him. "Yes," the man replied, "It's my name." The attendant looked at him and said softly: "Your name is not here. You must be alive. Go home and get on with your life." That was the word he needed. He was indeed alive, and he went home and went on to become a better man, a better husband, a better father.

This is the message the Christian faith has for you and me today: "You are alive; get on with your life and mission." The Spirit is a gift of pulse; it brings the gift of life.

3. Third, the Gift of the Spirit Is the Gift of Purpose

Look again at the final words of Jesus: "You shall receive power when the Holy Spirit has come upon you; and you shall be my witnesses in Jerusalem and in all Judea and Samaria and to the end of the earth" (RSV). The coming of the Holy Spirit instilled in the church its mission and ministry. Our purpose is to be Christ's witnesses throughout all the world.

The continued growth of the church and the proclamation of the gospel is dependent upon us. The gospel is no longer dependent upon Peter, James, John, Paul, and Silas, and all of those early Christians. It is dependent upon each one of us in our life and witness. It is an awesome task and an incredible responsibility, but remember we are not alone in this. The Spirit is always with us, and that's what keeps us going.

There is an old legend that emphasizes this point. The

story tells of Jesus' return to heaven after his time on earth and the angels gather to hear his account of what happened there on earth. Jesus tells them about his miracles, his teachings and then tells of the pain of his arrest, trial and crucifixion, and of the glory of resurrection. When Jesus finished his account, one of the angels asks Jesus, "But what happens now?" Jesus said: "I have left behind eleven faithful disciples and a handful of men and women who have faithfully followed me. They will declare my message, express my love, and build my church. They will share and witness to the faith to their friends, and they will share with theirs until the whole world will know their story and the gospel." But the angel said, what if they fail? Or, what if at some point in history the people of the church fail or cease their witness? What is the alternative plan? Jesus answered: "I have no other plan. I am depending upon them." The gift of the Spirit is the gift of purpose and mission.

4. Finally, the Gift of the Spirit Is the Gift of Power

Our purpose is rather overwhelming when you really think about it. Sometimes we feel like Lou Holtz, who once said, "I know the Lord does not put on us more than we can stand, but sometimes I think he overestimates my ability."

The thought of the future of the church and gospel in our hands may seem to be an overestimate of our ability; but the key is that we do not do it alone. Jesus said, "You will receive power!"

Pentecost is about power, the coming of the Spirit to empower the church to fulfill its purpose and calling.

The book of Acts is the story of this power in the lives of the disciples and the new church. Peter is an example of the power of the Spirit in a life. He was the one who denied Jesus in the crisis moment of his life. But following Pentecost, we meet a new Peter, one who preaches boldly and performs miracles in the name of Jesus. When told to quit preaching and teaching in Jesus' name, Peter responded with great courage and fearlessness: "I must obey God rather than man" (Acts 5:29, paraphrased). He had received the gift of power.

Paul in writing to the Corinthians shared his experience with this unique power of the Spirit:

> Therefore, having this ministry by the mercy of God, we do not lose heart. . . . But we have this treasure in earthen vessels, to show that the transcendent power belongs to God and not to us. We are afflicted in every way, but not crushed; perplexed, but not driven to despair; persecuted, but not forsaken; struck down, but not destroyed. . . . So we do not lose heart. (2 Cor 4:1, 7-9, 16 RSV)

As I thought of Paul's statement, I remembered a story that was told at a California graduation. The speaker told about a young man who had received his diploma in 1974 and ten years later, the graduate sent his diploma back to the university saying that the degree had not helped him obtain employment in his chosen field or work. The speaker, who was the former chancellor of the university, said that he sent the diploma back to the young man and told him to keep it, that he had earned it. He went on to explain that the purpose of the university was to develop students who will be self-sufficient and involved with society, but what stuck with me was his statement to the young man: "It is not the purpose of a university to guarantee victory in life, but to equip one for the struggles of life."

That is the purpose of the church as well. It is not the purpose of the faith to guarantee us victory, success, or immunity from trouble. The purpose of the church is to equip us with the power to face the struggles of life.

That Greek word for spirit, *pneuma* (meaning "air" or "breath"), is the root word from which we get pneumatic tires—tires filled with air. The significant thing for me is that this reminds us that things filled with air consistently bounce up when thrown down, or, if in water, float, not able to be kept under, but always rising to the surface. That is also true of things filled with the Holy Spirit of God, the *pneuma*. They cannot be held down, they have the power to continually and consistently bounce up and rise again. Pentecost is the gift of power, the power to be a witness and the power to face the struggles of life.

At the Wesleyan Chapel in Nottingham, England, where William Booth, founder of The Salvation Army was converted, there is a memorial plaque that members of The Salvation Army from all over the world come to see. They come out of respect for the man whose passion for the lost and lonely led him to start this movement.

One day, it is reported, an elderly man wearing the uniform of The Salvation Army came and stood in front of the memorial. He asked a minister standing nearby, "Can a man say his prayers here?" The minister assured him that he could. The old man dropped to his knees and, lifting his hands toward heaven, prayed in a fervent voice: "O Lord, do it again!"

As we seek to fulfill our mission to be witnesses for Christ in our world today, we also pray, "O Lord, do it again." Send us the gift of the Holy Spirit, a gift of presence, a gift of pulse and life, a gift of purpose, and a gift of power. So, a good prayer for us to pray today could well be: "Lord, send me your spirit and please send it to me right now."

CHAPTER NINE

Lord, Give Me a Sense of Urgency

SCRIPTURE: 2 TIMOTHY 4:6-13

Some years ago when we were living in Shreveport, a doctor came to see me one Thursday morning. His face was radiant. I could tell he was excited about something.

"Jim," he said, "I want to tell you something you don't know about me. I'm an alcoholic, and yesterday was a big day for me." He said, "It was my fifteenth anniversary of sobriety. I haven't had a drink now for fifteen years. I feel so good, and things are just going so great for me and my family and my career. I owe it all to your good friend Dr. Tom Shipp. Fifteen years ago," he said, "I was living in Dallas and going to Lovers Lane United Methodist Church there, and Tom Shipp was my pastor. At the time, my life was an absolute mess. I was addicted to alcohol. I was drinking so heavily that I was about to lose everything. My family, my career, my friendships, and my health were all being destroyed by my drinking problems."

"Then," he said, "I hit bottom and I went to Tom Shipp, and he was great. He helped me so much. He got me involved in A.A. He helped my family. He brought me back to God. He turned it around for me." He said, "I owe Tom so much, and as soon as we finish our visit, I'm going to get in my car and drive to Dallas, and I'm going to tell Tom Shipp what I've wanted to tell him for fifteen years—how indebted I am to him, how grateful I am to him, how he was so instrumental by the grace of God in turning my life around. For fifteen years I have wanted to say *thank you* to Tom Shipp, and today I am going to do it!" "Oh, Doctor," I said to him, "you haven't heard. I'm sorry to tell you this, but Tom Shipp had a heart attack in a church meeting last week, and he died."

I will never forget the look on the doctor's face as he realized that he had waited too long. But the truth is that we can all relate to that, can't we? We all know the feeling of putting off and putting off, of procrastinating and waiting too long.

- How many letters have never been written?

- How many phone calls have never been made?
- How many compliments have been left unsaid?
- How many *I'm sorry's* remain unspoken?
- How many *thank you's* have never been uttered?
- How many *I love you's* are still unexpressed?
- How many commitments are still not made because we waited too long?

Now that brings us to this scripture lesson in 2 Timothy. Let me set this passage in context. The Apostle Paul had known Timothy for some years. Paul was the one who had led Timothy to know Jesus Christ. Paul had known Timothy's mother, and over the years had trained Timothy in the faith and had taken Timothy along with him on his missionary journeys. It is pretty certain that 2 Timothy was one of the last things Paul ever wrote. He wrote it while in prison, not long before he was executed by the Romans. Paul knew when he wrote these words that his days on this earth were numbered.

Paul was in prison in Rome and Timothy was in Ephesus, so Paul writes and asks Timothy to come to see him as soon as he can—and to bring his cloak (to warm his body), his books (to warm his mind), and his parchments (the Scriptures to warm his soul). Then Paul says this to Timothy: "Do your best to come before winter" (2 Tim 4:21).

Now the question is, did Timothy come? Did he actually get there before the Apostle Paul died? The truth is we don't know. The Bible never says. Church history never says. But let me ask you something: would you have gone? If Paul wrote to you and said, "Come and come quickly; I don't have much time left. I really need to see you before I die. Please come and bring my coat and my books and especially my Bible. I need your support and companionship." Would you have gone, or would you have procrastinated?

This phrase, "Come before winter," became the title of one of the most famous sermons ever preached in America. It was preached thirty-seven times from the pulpit of First Presbyterian Church in Pittsburgh, Pennsylvania, by Clarence Edward McCartney, one of the great preachers of the twentieth century. After he preached it the first time, the church members were so moved that they called a special meeting of their church board and mandated that every year Clarence McCartney would preach that sermon again. They wanted to hear that sermon every year, and for thirty-seven years, every year, Clarence McCartney preached that sermon!

Now, in that sermon Clarence McCartney painted a powerful image by raising this question: What if Timothy had delayed? What if he didn't go immediately? What if he said, "Of course I'll go, but I've got a lot of stuff going on right now. I'll go, but a little later." And then when he gets down to the dock some time later, they said, "Sorry. It's too late. It's wintertime now. It's too cold. The sea is too rough. Can't go now. Wait till after winter." When spring comes, Timothy goes down and takes the first ship to Rome and he gets there and he is wondering, "Am I in time?"

Clarence McCartney imagined this amazing scene where Timothy goes to the prison and says to the jailer, "I'm here to see the Apostle Paul." And the jailer says, "You must be Timothy. You haven't heard—Paul was executed last winter." And the jailer said, "Timothy, he was looking for you. Every day, every time when I would go to his cell to take him his meal, he would always say, 'Timothy, is that you?' 'Is this Timothy?' 'Has Timothy come?' And when Paul died, the last words he said were, 'Tell Timothy, my beloved son in the faith, that I love him . . . and I always will throughout all eternity.'"

Now, how would you feel if you were Timothy, and you hadn't made it in time? We can all relate to that, can't we? We all know the feeling of putting off and putting off and putting off, and then it's too late. I'm not trying to lay a heavy guilt trip on us but rather to simply raise this question for us to grapple with a bit. What is God asking you to do? What is the thing God is calling you to do right now in your life? What step is God asking you to take? Let me prime the pump of your thinking about this with three thoughts.

1. First of All, If You Need to Say, "I'm Sorry" to Someone, Do It Now

In the Sermon on the Mount, Jesus says if you come to the altar and remember that you are at odds with someone first, go be reconciled and then come back to the altar (Matt 5:23-24). And you know full well what he is talking about, don't you? You see someone coming toward you, and your first inclination is to look the other way or to cross the street so you don't have to face him or her. Or perhaps it is that relationship in your group, in your neighborhood, in your home, in your workplace, that has grown cold or distant or hostile or sour. You are working in the same office, living on the same street, sharing the same bed, but the relationship is chilly, cold, tense, strained, heavy.

What are you waiting for? Why don't you fix that? Oh, but you said, "It's not my fault." Of course it's not your fault, but as a Christian, it is your responsibility. Listen! Broken relationships are just too painful, too stressful, too debilitating, and too destructive. They bring ulcers, headaches, insomnia, loneliness, and bitterness. What a way to live! It's no way to live!

So if you are at odds with any other person right now, please don't let that broken relationship fester any longer. Don't let it poison your spirit or paralyze your soul. For their sake, for your sake, for God's sake, go fix it; go make peace. Say, "I'm sorry and I want things to be right with us." Go and God will go with you.

2. Second, If You Need to Say, "I Love You" to Someone, Do It Now

Have you heard about the man whose wife suddenly died? They had been married for more than forty years. Two days later after her funeral, he stood at her gravesite and stared at her coffin. Blinking back the tears, he said, "She was the light of my life. She brought such joy to our home. She did everything for me. She was the perfect wife and companion. I loved her so much, and once I almost told her!" Isn't that sad? Isn't that pitiful? "Once I almost told her."

One of the most tragic things in the world is to go through life not feeling loved and accepted and re-spected. Another "quiet tragedy" is going through life loving someone and yet never telling them. The point is, some things are so urgent, so vital, so crucial, and life can sometimes be so fragile, that we must not; we dare not put them off. The point is obvious: if you need to say, "I'm sorry" to someone; or if you need to say, "I love you" to someone, what are you waiting for? Do it now!

3. Third, If You Need to Say Yes to God, Do It Now

Have you heard about the man who was asked, "How are your children doing in school these days?" "Well, they are doing better," he replied. "But I do still go to PTA meetings under an assumed name!" Many parents can relate to that and understand that, and obviously that dad was just kidding. But the truth is, God is the opposite of that. He openly claims us. He openly seeks us out. He openly reaches out to us. He openly, intentionally, graciously, relentlessly, sacrificially offers gifts to us:

- The gift of salvation
- The gift of forgiveness
- The gift of eternal life
- The gift of Christ
- The gift of his unconditional love.

But we have to do our part. We have to accept the gift. What are we waiting for? Why do we hold back? Why are we hesitant to accept God's gracious gift of himself? Why are we so reluctant to say yes to God?

In the summer of 1984, I was attending the Jurisdictional Conference in Lubbock. In one of the early ballots (as was expected), my predecessor, Dr. Walter Underwood, was elected bishop. That election did two things: it provided the church with a great new bishop, and it opened up the best Methodist church in America, St. Luke's United Methodist Church in Houston. During the recesses and breaks at the Jurisdictional Conference, I would stand around with my minister friends and we would talk about "Who is going to follow Walter at St. Luke's?" My friends mentioned a long list of names—mine was not one of them! But then I ran into Bishop Ben Oliphint and he said to me, "Jim, your name is on the St. Luke's list, and I think there is a good chance that you could end up there."

Some weeks later, word came to me that my name had made it to the short list. About this time, a minister friend of mine who was a seasoned veteran minister in Texas called me one night, and he said, "Jim, it's not my style to give advice, but I've called tonight to give you some good advice. Are you listening to me?"

"Yes, sir," I responded.

"OK. Here it is. If they offer you St. Luke's, don't ask to see the parsonage! Don't ask what the salary is! Don't ask anything! Just say yes! Do you hear me, young man?"

"Yes, sir."

"Can you say yes?"

"Yes, sir!"

"OK, that's all you have to do. Just say yes."

And then he hung up.

Now, of course, I did say yes and as they say, the rest is history. But you know, I've thought about that older minister's advice a lot, and he was right. And that's the advice I want to pass on to you. God is offering you his love. Don't ask any questions. Just say yes! And God is calling you to do something and you know what it is—to join the church, to teach that class, to sing in the choir, to work with the children or youth, to make a pledge, to get in that Bible study, to commit your life to Christ. You know what it is.

Well, what are you waiting for? Why are you putting it off? What's the holdup? Do it now; do it today! Do it this moment! Accept God's call! Accept His gift of love. Just say yes. Come to God before winter.

If you need to say, "I'm sorry," "I love you," "Yes" to God, don't procrastinate any longer. Don't put it off anymore—life is too short, too fragile. Just do it now! So, this is a good prayer for us to pray today: "Lord, give me a sense of urgency and please, God, give it to me right now!"

CHAPTER TEN

Lord, Give Me Healing

Scripture: Luke 10:30-37

There is a scene in one of the *Peanuts* cartoons where Lucy screams at Charlie Brown: "I don't care if I ever see you again! Do you hear me?" Charlie Brown is devastated by the attack. Linus comes by and says: "She really hurt your feelings, didn't she, Charlie Brown? I hope she didn't take all the life out of you." Charlie responds: "No, not completely, but you can number me among the walking wounded!"

We know what Charlie Brown is talking about, because all of us sometimes number ourselves among the walking wounded. Many people hide their wounds and on the surface of life all seems well, but they are wounded nonetheless. Longfellow's wife died a tragic death, and months later he wrote in his diary: "Though outwardly I appear calm, inwardly, I bleed." Even that person you think has it all together may be one of the walking wounded.

Ernest Hemingway in *A Farewell to Arms* writes: "The world breaks everyone, then some become strong at the broken places." Jesus in the parable of the foundations reminds us that there is no escape from the problems, hurts, and storms of life. They are a part of the human scene and the dynamic of human relationships. A modern-day theologian and pastor, Henri Nouwen, who writes from the perspective of a "wounded healer," speaks of the wounds of life with words such as "alienation, separation, isolation, and loneliness." We all know firsthand about the wounds, heartbreaks, and shattered dreams in these frustrating disappointments. Some people know dramatically the pain of rejection, failure, verbal abuse, divorce, grief, and sorrow.

And sometimes it seems that no one understands or cares. In reading Jesus' parable of the Good Samaritan, many people in our world today relate quickly to the victim in the story, beaten, left bleeding, and unable to cry out. And people who should care pass by and offer no help or understanding. But let me hurry to say that the good news for them and for us is that God is the Good Samaritan to a wounded world. God is aware of our hurts and the wounds of our life. Listen to the words of the psalmist: "The LORD is near to the brokenhearted," "He heals the brokenhearted, / and binds up their wounds" (34:18; 147:3).

The prophet Isaiah speaking of the Messiah described him as having the Spirit of the Lord upon him and being anointed to bring good news to the afflicted and to bind up the brokenhearted. When Jesus opened his public ministry in Nazareth, he read this passage from Isaiah and proclaimed its fulfillment in him. His ministry was to bind up and heal the wounds of our life. In the Good Samaritan parable, Jesus shows us that love is the ability to see the wounded and those in need and to have compassion on them and bind up their wounds. When we hear the great promise of the Scriptures that God is love, we can know that a big part of what that means is that God knows, God understands, God cares, and God heals.

Shortly after my mother's accidental death in an automobile accident several years ago, my sister, Susie, wrote me a letter, and in it she shared this quote someone had given to her. "God will mend a broken heart, if we will give him all the pieces."

Let me suggest to you how we can deal with our woundedness and allow God to bind our wounds and heal our broken hearts.

1. First of All, We Accept the Reality of Our Wounds

Because God is with us, we can be realistic about our life. God empowers us to accept and face whatever it is that has wounded our life. Real wounds do not go away because we ignore them or suppress them; they only surface in more destructive and dangerous ways later.

Some years ago, Pat Conroy dealt with just this issue in his popular novel *The Prince of Tides*, which was also made into a movie. It is the story of a dysfunctional family and of an especially traumatic event that occurred in their lives. Tragically, they are forced to live and act as if this event never occurred, and this repressed wound acts destructively upon them for the rest of their lives. It finally comes to a head when the daughter in the family tries to commit suicide and cannot remember what has pushed her to do it. Her brother, through a psychiatrist, becomes her memory; and through a long process of dragging up and facing the wounds of the past, not only is the girl healed, but so is her brother. In helping her, he also helps himself. It is a great, moving story, but it reminds all of us that the first step in any problem or hurt is the power and willingness to face it, to get it out in the open and deal with it. Surrounded and assured of God's unconditional love, we can do this.

Some things in life are not going to change, and we must learn to live with them and to live through them. Paul had something in his life that he referred to as "a thorn in the flesh." He prayed and prayed about it, but it did not go away. He had to live with it and through it. Jesus had to live with and through the cross. The early Christians had to live through persecution. There are some things, some people, and some wounds that we have to live with and through. Reinhold Niebuhr in his "Serenity Prayer" expressed it like this: "O God, give me the serenity to accept what cannot be changed, the courage to change what should be changed, and the wisdom to distinguish the one from the other."

2. Second, We Lean on God's Power and Strength

One of the things Paul learned in his struggles with his thorn in the flesh was that this wound and weakness made him rely more upon God. He said: "Whenever I am weak, then I am strong" (2 Cor 12:10).

Lloyd Ogilvie in one of his books writes about brokenheartedness and says: "Brokenness builds. . . . Whatever happens that breaks us open to a deeper invasion of the Lord's spirit is a blessing in disguise." When the wounds of our life seem almost more than we can bear; when we lose a loved one, or a vital relationship disintegrates, or we feel all alone and forsaken, or we have been the victim of unjust criticism and condemnation, or we experience the breakup of our home by divorce; these are times when we do not have the resources, the strength and power to cope or go on. We have to lean on God, trust God to bring us through it, and keep us going.

When Jesus was on the cross in the depths of his suffering, he looked up to God and said, "Father, into your hands I commend my spirit" (Luke 23:46). As God's children we can do the same. In the midst of our moments of suffering, we too can commend our spirit and life into the hands of God. A poet puts it like this:

> I think what kept keeping on
> When I could not, was God.

This is the good news of the Christian faith. We can lean on God for strength and healing!

3. Third, We Can Hold on to Hope

Hope is a necessity for real living, but especially in the wounded moment. As Christians, we can have the hope and expectation that life will be good again. It may not be the same, but it can be good again. Hope is belief in possibility. It is not some unrealistic optimism that everything will work out and things will be like they were before. It is the confidence and faith that however things turn out, God will be with us, will see us through, and will bring healing.

Hope comes out of a resurrection faith, the faith that no matter how bad things get, God is in the midst working with us for good. That's what Paul was saying in Romans: "In everything God works for good" (8:28 RSV).

In the worst moments in the life of Israel, facing the Red Sea with the Egyptians in pursuit, in the midst of the destruction of Jerusalem, in the time of exile in Babylon, and under the heel of the Roman Empire, the word from God was always to hold on to your hope, God will save. And the Psalmist expressed it like this: "Why art thou cast down, O my soul? and why art thou disquieted within me? hope in God" (Ps 43:5 KJV). The overwhelming word of the Bible is that God is *hesed*, steadfast love, incredibly dependable, a God who will not forsake us or let us down in the crunch. Hold on to your hope!

4. Fourth, We Can Get in or Stay in a Healing Community

The church is God's healing community. We are not created to be alone; we were made for community and family. The Bible speaks of the power and strength of community, especially a holy community. We give and draw strength from one another.

One of the tragedies that I have noted over the years is that too often the wounded tend to draw away from the church rather than to it. But those who hang in with their church feel a strength, concern, and a loving, healing touch they can get nowhere else.

Some years ago in a church I was serving, two of our most active members suddenly separated and got a divorce. The man left the church, but the woman continued to come and serve. One morning I received a letter from her. She wrote: "I want to share with you how much the support of the church folk has meant to me these last four months. I guess I had rather taken this support as expected until the other night at a family services class I'm taking for separated and divorced women. At that time, I listened to two other women, who said they had to change their church memberships because they felt ostracized and totally left out of all their church functions. I was very shocked and told them how I had felt nothing but love and support from our church and could not have made it without my church and its love."

5. Finally, We Can Give Ourselves to a Cause Greater than Ourselves and Become Wounded Healers

There comes a time, if we are to be healed, that we turn our attention away from our wounds and focus on something greater than ourselves. Many wounds do not heal because we continuously irritate them by constant examination. If we want to be healed, it helps to forget about ourselves and our wounds for a while and lose ourselves in helping, serving, and caring for others.

It is not surprising in *The Prince of Tides* that when the brother reaches out in love to his troubled twin sister and begins the painful journey into the past for her sake, he not only helps her, but in the process finds hope and healing for himself. In losing ourselves in love, for the kingdom and others, we find ourselves and our life.

Karl Menninger was asked: "Suppose you suspect that you're heading for a nervous breakdown. What should you do?"

Menninger answered: "Go straight to your front door, turn the knob, cross the tracks, and find somebody who needs you."

If Hemingway is right and the world breaks everyone, then we all have the opportunity to be what Henri Nouwen calls "wounded healers." Because we know what it is like to be wounded, we can understand, help, and be an instrument in God's healing.

Have you ever wondered why the Samaritan, rather than the priest and Levite, stopped and helped the man who was the victim of the thieves on the Jericho Road. I think it was more than just for the shock factor of a

Samaritan doing good. I think the Samaritan knew what it was like to be wounded. He knew what it was like for no one to care. He knew what it was like to be ignored and discriminated against. He could identify with the victim, and his heart went out to him. Out of the Samaritan's own woundedness he helped, and I would imagine that it may have made his own wounds a little more bearable. The poet put it well in these powerful words:

We cannot heal unless we love them much,
For only sorrow, sorrow understands.

Do this and I think you will discover that my sister's friend was right: if we give God all the pieces, God will mend our broken hearts and heal our wounds. So, our prayer for today could well be: "Lord, give me healing and give it to me right now."

CHAPTER ELEVEN

Lord, Give Me Childlikeness

SCRIPTURE: MATTHEW 18:1-4

William Griffin in his book *Jesus for Children* tells of an exchange between Jesus and Judas concerning the children who are always following them and trying to get to Jesus. Judas tells Jesus, "You don't have enough time to sleep. You don't have enough time to pray. Why do you spend so much time with those noisy children?"

Jesus answers, "Because they are fun! And heaven is a lot like a playground. Unless you remember what it is like to be a child, you won't get in." To which Judas says, "Does that mean I have to hop, skip, and jump forever?" And Jesus answers, "No, it means you have to be curious and eager and good and honest and fair."

An eighty-year-old woman from the hill country of Kentucky was once asked to look back over her life and reflect on what she had learned. With a kind of wistfulness she began, "If I had it to do over, if I had my life to live over, I would relax more, I would be sillier; I would take fewer things seriously, I would eat more ice cream, and go barefoot earlier in the spring. You see, I'm one of those people who live seriously and sanely hour after hour, day after day. I've been one of those persons who never went anyplace without a thermometer, a hot water bottle, a raincoat, and a parachute. If I had it to do again, I'd travel lighter."

Both of these stories highlight and dramatize the point of the text for this chapter. In Matthew 18, Jesus underscores the importance of the childlike spirit. He says that if we are to enter the kingdom of heaven, we must become like a little child and great are those who do.

The story begins with a question about greatness. Jesus answers the question in a most unusual way. He does not speak about greatness in terms of what we have, or what we achieve, or who we know, or where we live. He surprises and, perhaps, stuns the disciples by using a child as an example of greatness.

In our time, we would think that what Jesus did with the child was cute and sweet, but in Jesus' time, it was astonishing and outrageous. Children in the first century were regarded as naïve, uneducated, foolishly inferior, and without status or rights. Children were under the total domination of their father. Fred Craddock describes the child as "the classic symbol of the powerless, those without claim or value in the society of the day." This ancient child was humble, loyal, dependent, and obedient to the father. A child as the symbol of greatness was shocking to them.

So, what did Jesus have in mind when he called disciples of yesterday and today to become like little children? What does it mean to achieve greatness through being childlike? Many concepts and characteristics come quickly into our minds. Children are teachable, reachable, eager with wonder, adventurous, wanting to grow and learn, curious, dependent, loving, and trusting.

Jesus gives us a clue to what he means here in Matthew 18 as he associates humility with childlikeness. In our text Jesus says, "Whoever humbles himself like this child, he is the greatest in the kingdom of heaven" (v. 4 RSV). But when we observe and experience children, our normal ideas of humility aren't there.

Children aren't always modest; they are often proud of themselves. Children don't put themselves down; they usually feel good about themselves, if we let them. Children aren't overly serious and overly religious; they enjoy life, taking it lightly, and can laugh at themselves.

The kind of humility Jesus saw in children was that they know they don't know everything and are eager to learn and grow. They know they can't do everything and are dependent upon others. They know they don't have everything and are open to receive. Children believe easily, love generously, and live happily!

Jesus calls us to be more childlike in our lives, in our faith, and in our pursuit of happiness. So with that in mind, let me bring this closer to home with three thoughts:

1. First of All, Children Have the Ability to Celebrate and Embrace Life

Young children have a joy about life, an excitement about each day, and a sense of expectancy about the future. We adults, as we grow older, often lose that joy, excitement, and expectancy. Jesus calls us to recapture this attitude about life.

Robert Fulghum, in his book *All I Really Need to Know I Learned in Kindergarten*, shares his experience of visiting college campuses where people are at the end of their formal education process. He compares them with children in kindergarten, who are at the beginning of their educational process. Their answer to anything you ask them to do is yes! They are confident in spirit, eager to learn, and they believe that everything is still possible for them. But, says Fulghum, if you ask a college audience the same questions: "Can you draw? Can you sing? Can you dance?" Only a small percentage of hands will go up and even those will qualify their answer in some way. "I only sing in groups or I draw but not very well or I only slow dance or fast dance." What happened between kindergarten and college? They lost the childlike ability to celebrate and embrace life. We become cautious, timid, and undaring.

At my niece's wedding reception a few years ago, when the band started to play, our granddaughters and our great niece began to dance together, all three of them. They were totally uninhibited and danced the whole time. They enjoyed the reception more than anyone else. They celebrated life and embraced the moment.

That's what Jesus wants us to do—become like a little child; ease up, reach out, embrace each moment, celebrate life, and you will be great and so will your life!

2. Second, Children Have the Ability to Maintain a Sense of Wonder and Reverence for Life and the World

At this same wedding, the women of our family attended the bridesmaids' luncheon and the men were in charge of the children. There were our five grandchildren and our great niece and great nephew. We took them outside the motel where we were staying so they could play. They tossed Frisbees and ran and played together. In the midst of their play one of them discovered a bug. It was just a roly-poly bug, but they all stopped what they were doing to observe and examine this little bug. They were fascinated and filled with wonder looking at a bug. Soon after, someone found a four-leaf clover, and you would have thought they had found a hundred-dollar bill. Everyone had to look for a four-leaf clover. It was exciting to them. Life still had a sense of wonder and reverence for them, even for the simplest of God's creation.

Jesus says we need to have that kind of approach and attitude about life. We need to see life's blessings all around us and within us and one another. To become childlike is to stand before our world and before God's grace and love with a sense of acceptance, wonder, and reverence. In this attitude is the spark of life.

3. Third and Finally, Children Have the Ability to Be Trusting and Obedient

The child that Jesus had in mind was trusting and obedient, which is the characteristic children of God of all ages need in our relationship to our Heavenly Father. A little child is ever trusting; this is the means through which they learn about all things.

They trust what we teach them; they implicitly believe us and in us. Jesus wants us to have that kind of trust in God.

A little girl had somehow received a bad cut in the soft flesh of her eyelid. The doctor knew that some stitches were needed, but he also knew that because of the location of the cut he should not use an anesthetic. He talked with the little girl, and he told her what he must do. He asked her if she thought she could stand the touch of the needle without jumping. She thought for a moment and then said simply, "I think I can if Daddy will hold me while you do it."

So the father took his little girl in his lap, steadied her against his shoulder and held her tightly in his arms. The surgeon then quickly did his work and sewed up the cut in her eyelid. The little girl, safe in her father's arms, did not flinch. She trusted him! To become like a little child is to trust and obey.

Andrew Gilles wrote a poignant poem about a father and son praying together one night. First, the little boy confesses some little something that he had done that he felt was wrong, and then the little boy asked God to forgive him and to make him good and strong and wise like his daddy. Then the little boy dozed off into a peaceful sleep. Touched and inspired by the beautiful faith of his son, the father then falls on his knees by the little boy's bed and prays, "O God, make me a child like my child here / Pure, guileless, trusting Thee with faith sincere."

Unless you become like a little child, you cannot enter the kingdom of heaven. So, our prayer today could well be: "Lord, please give me a childlike spirit and give it to me right now."

CHAPTER TWELVE

Lord, Give Me Compassion

SCRIPTURE: MARK 5:21-43

A business executive became depressed. Things were not going well at work, and he was bringing his problems home with him every night. Every evening he would eat his dinner in silence, shutting out his wife and five-year-old daughter. Then he would go into the den and read the paper, using the newspaper to wall his family out of his life.

After several nights of this, one evening his daughter took her little hand and pushed the newspaper down. She then jumped into her father's lap, wrapped her arms around his neck, and hugged him strongly. The father said abruptly, "Honey, you are hugging me to death!" "No, Daddy," the little girl said, "I'm hugging you to life!"

This was the greatness of Jesus. He took people where they were and hugged them to life. That is precisely what we see Jesus doing here in this dramatic passage in Mark 5. He is loving needy and hurting people, hugging them to life. This passage is a fascinating one because here we have a story within a story—or two healing stories rolled into one—and the people involved could not be more different.

On the one hand, as we saw in chapter 2, Jairus and his family represented the elite of society in those days. Jairus was a powerful and influential man in the community, and he and his family would have been respected members of the high-society group in the city. But that day they were in deep despair because Jairus's twelve-year-old daughter, the apple of his eye, was terribly sick and dying.

On the other hand, the hemorrhaging woman in the crowd was a social outcast. She was considered unclean as one who was under the judgment of God, and therefore not allowed to set foot in the synagogue. In this magnificent passage, these two vastly different people— the down and out hemorrhaging woman and the upper-crust daughter of Jairus—are loved into life by our Lord. Remember the story with me.

Jesus and his disciples had been going from town to town. He had been preaching the gospel and healing people. Large crowds were coming out. They were clamoring to see Jesus and hear him. One day this man called Jairus came looking for Jesus. Jairus was the ruler of the synagogue. He fell down at the feet of Jesus and begged the Master to come to his house because his only daughter (who was about twelve years of age) was gravely ill and dying. Jesus agreed to go with him and as they went, people began to press in around Jesus. The people were so excited to be near the master that they were pushing and shoving and crowding in close to him.

In the crowd that day was a woman who had been hemorrhaging for twelve years. She had tried everything she knew to try, but no luck—no relief, no help for her problem. No one had been able to cure her. She slipped up behind Jesus, working her way through the crowd—and when no one seemed to be looking, she reached out tentatively, fearfully, and touched the hem of his robe. At once, the hemorrhaging stopped. For the first time in twelve years, the flow of blood stopped.

Jesus simultaneously felt or sensed that something special had happened. It was a unique touch, and he felt strength go out of him. Immediately, Jesus stopped. He turned around and asked, "Who touched me?" The disciples were astonished by the question in the midst of all the pushing and shoving and jostling.

"What do you mean, 'who touched you?' Everybody's touching you."

But, you see, they couldn't tell a push from a touch. Jesus could! He knew the difference, and he knew that it was a tender touch that had drawn strength out of him. The woman had not expected to be detected, but when Jesus turned and asked that question, she knew that he knew. She came forward trembling, fell at his feet, and confessed that she was the one who had touched the hem of his garment. She explained in a rush of words why she had touched Jesus and how she had been instantly cured. Graciously, Jesus lifted her up and said to her, "Daughter, your faith has made you well; go in peace."

Notice how gentle and loving Jesus is with her as he gives her a new lease on life. He doesn't chastise her for interrupting him. He doesn't critique her theology or her superstitious expectations. Jesus doesn't rebuke her for seeing him as a sort of last resort. Rather, he gives her act the most gracious possible reception. And although we know the healing came from Jesus, he humbly gives her the credit: "Your faith has made you well," he says to her.

Now, the rest of the story is even more remarkable. Word comes that Jairus's daughter has died. Jairus is devastated by the news, but Jesus encourages him and tells him to keep on believing. Together, they go on to Jarius's home. Already, mourners are there, lamenting the tragic loss of the little girl, but Jesus goes right into the house and heals her, resurrects her. He brings the little girl back to life, and you will remember that he then tells the people in the house to give her something to eat.

Now, of course, there are many beautiful lessons here in Mark 5 in these two dramatic stories of healing, and we could go off now in any number of directions. But my focus is on the power of compassion and the amazing, incredible things compassion can accomplish when it is given and when it is received.

1. First of All, Compassion Has the Power to Heal

Scientific research is now confirming what many of us have suspected all along—that loving compassion plays a big part in the healing of a hurting body. Compassion has the power to heal physically, emotionally, and spiritually.

Have you heard the legend of the Fisher King? When the Fisher King was a boy, he was sent out to spend the night alone in the forest as a test of his courage to be king. During the night, he had a vision of the Holy Grail (the cup used by our Lord at the Last Supper), surrounded by great flames of fire. Immediately, he became excited by the prospect of wealth and glory that would be his by possessing such a great prize. Greedily, he reached into the flames to grab the Holy Grail, but the flames were too much and he was severely wounded.

As the years went by, the Fisher King became more despondent and alone, and his wound grew deeper. One day the Fisher King, feeling sad and depressed and in pain, went for a walk in the forest. He came upon a court jester. "Are you all right?" the jester asked. "Is there anything I can do for you? Anything at all?" "Well, I am very thirsty," the Fisher King replied. The jester took an old, dilapidated cup from the bag, filled it with water from a nearby stream, and gave it to the Fisher King. As the Fisher King drank, he suddenly felt his wound healing for the first time. And incredibly the old cup he was drinking from had turned into the Holy Grail. "What wonderful magic do you possess?" the Fisher King asked the jester. The jester just shrugged and said, "I know no magic. All I did was get a drink for a thirsty soul."

This old legend underscores a great truth that is written large in the Scriptures, namely this: greed and selfishness bring pain and suffering, but love and compassion bring healing and life. We see it here in Mark 5 as Jesus reaches out to the hemorrhaging woman and the daughter of Jairus: compassion has the power to heal.

2. Second, Compassion Has the Power to Reconcile

This is why Jesus insisted that the one who had touched the hem of his garment come forward. This woman was considered ceremonially unclean. She was not permitted to set foot in the synagogue. She was a social outcast. Jesus wanted to make it clear to everyone that she was well. Jesus not only healed her but also restored her to an active place in normal society. He reconciled her with the community.

In his book *The Preaching Event*, John Claypool tells a poignant story about identical twin brothers who never married because they enjoyed each other's company so much. When their father died, they took over his store and ran it together in a joyful collaboration. But one day a man came in to make a small purchase and paid for it with a dollar. The brother who made the sale placed the dollar on top of the cash register and walked the customer to the door to say goodbye. When he returned, the dollar bill was gone. He said to his twin brother, "Did you take the dollar bill I left here?" "No, I didn't," answered the brother. "Surely you took it," he said. "There was nobody else in the store." The brother became angry: "I'm telling you, I did not take the dollar bill."

From that point, mistrust and suspicion grew until finally the two brothers could not work together. They put a partition right down the middle of the building and made it into two stores. In anger, they refused to speak for the next twenty years.

One day a stranger pulled up in a car and entered one of the two stores. "Have you been in business very long here?" the stranger asked. "Yes, thirty or forty years," was the answer. "Good," continued the stranger. "I very much need to tell you something. Some twenty years ago, I passed through this town. I was out of work and homeless. I jumped off a boxcar. I had no money and I had not eaten for days. I came down that alley outside and when I looked into your store window, I saw a dollar bill on the cash register. I slipped in and took it. Recently I became a Christian. I was converted and accepted Christ as my personal Savior. I know now it was wrong of me to steal that dollar bill, and I have come to pay you back with interest and to beg your forgiveness."

When the stranger finished his confession, the old storekeeper began to weep as he said, "Would you do me a favor? Would you please come next door and tell that story to my brother?" Of course, with the second telling, the two brothers were reconciled with many hugs and apologies and tears. Twenty years of hurt and a broken relationship were based not on fact but on mistrust and misunderstanding. But then healing came, reconciliation came, because of that stranger's love for Christ.

The point is clear: Christ is the Reconciler, but, as the Apostle Paul put it, we can be "agents of reconciliation" when we live in the spirit of love and compassion.

Compassion has the power to heal. Compassion has the power to reconcile.

3. Third and Finally, Compassion Has the Power to Redeem

Let me ask you something. Be honest now. Do you know the redeeming love of Christ in your life? Has he turned your life around? Has he loved you into life?

There is a beautiful old story about Zacchaeus the tax collector. It tells how in later years, he rose early every morning and left his house. His wife, curious, followed him one morning. At the town well he filled a bucket, and he walked until he came to a sycamore tree. There, setting down the bucket, he began to clean away the stones, the branches, and the rubbish from around the base of the tree. Having done that, he poured water on the roots and stood there in silence, gently caressing the trunk with both of his hands. When his amazed wife came out of hiding and asked what he was doing, Zacchaeus replied simply, "This is where I found Christ!"

I can just imagine that for the rest of their lives, both women, the woman who touched the hem of Jesus' robe that day on the street and the daughter of Jairus who was raised up in that room in her home, continually brought people back to those sacred spots and said, "This is where I found Christ! This is where Christ loved me into life!"

Do you have a sacred spot like that? This is the good news of our Christian faith, isn't it? Compassion has the power to heal, to reconcile, and to redeem. So, our prayer today might well be: "Lord, give me the spirit of compassion and please give it to me right now."

DISCUSSION GUIDE

for
Lord, Give Me Patience, and
Give It to Me Right Now!
BY JAMES W. MOORE AND BOB J. MOORE

JOHN D. SCHROEDER

1. Lord, Give Me Patience

Snapshot Summary

This chapter uses the story of the encounter of Jesus and the rich young ruler to show how the best things in life take time. It also illustrates the value of waiting or working for something.

Reflection/Discussion Questions

1. Reflect on/discuss your interest in this book and what you hope to gain from your reading and discussion of it.
2. Share a situation that required you to have patience.
3. Reflect on/discuss what it means to be a patient person and the value of having patience.
4. What lessons can we learn from the encounter of Jesus and the rich young ruler?
5. Name some significant accomplishments that take time.

6. What is the value in waiting or working for something?
7. Reflect on/discuss the challenges and the benefits of developing a meaningful prayer life.
8. Name some of the keys toward gaining a better understanding of Scripture.
9. What does it mean to be a real, committed church person? Describe this person.
10. What additional thoughts or ideas from this chapter would you like to explore?

Activities

As a group: Create "patience cards" using blank index cards as carry-along reminders for being patient. The brief wording on the card could be an affirmation, a prayer, or some meaningful thought about patience. Share your patience cards with one another.

At home: Focus on being a more patient person this week, and work toward a more meaningful prayer life.

Prayer: *Dear God, thank you for reminding us of the power of patience. Help us value personal effort and sacrifice to achieve accomplishment. May we learn from the example of Jesus how to live better lives. Amen.*

2. Lord, Give Me Faith

Snapshot Summary

This chapter examines how faith, trust, and hope can work miracles.

Reflection/Discussion Questions

1. Share a time in your life when you needed to have faith.
2. Reflect on/discuss what it means to be a kind person. Give an example of a kindness shown to you.

3. How was Jairus changed by the illness of his daughter?
4. Name some qualities you admire in Jairus.
5. What does it mean to have an active faith? Describe such a faith.
6. Reflect on/discuss why faith needs to be hopeful.
7. Why can we always trust in Jesus?
8. Describe some situations that test a person's faith.
9. Reflect on/discuss some of the keys to building a stronger faith.
10. What additional thoughts or ideas from this chapter would you like to explore?

Activities

As a Group: If you were to illustrate faith, what would it look like? Draw a symbol or an illustration that shows what faith means to you. Share and explain your drawings.

At Home: Reread Luke 8:49-56, and remember the story of Jairus this week as you work to increase your faith.

Prayer: *Dear God, thank you for this opportunity to learn more about faith and what it means to trust you and to be a faithful Christian. Help us build a faith that is active and strong, a faith that connects us with you. Amen.*

3. Lord, Give Me Life

Snapshot Summary

This chapter is about adding life to our years through hope and healthy relationships with God and others.

Reflection/Discussion Questions

1. Reflect on/discuss what kind of life most people desire. What do people want from life?

2. How is Zacchaeus like many of us? Make a list of the similarities.
3. What lessons about life can we learn from the encounter between Jesus and Zacchaeus?
4. Reflect on/discuss the mission statement of Jesus. Why is it important?
5. How would you describe what it is like to have a healthy relationship with God?
6. List some keys to having a healthy relationship with God.
7. What does it mean to have a healthy regard for others? How is this accomplished?
8. Share a dark moment from the past when you needed hope.
9. Reflect on/discuss the importance of hope and having a hopeful outlook on life.
10. What additional thoughts or ideas from this chapter would you like to explore?

Activities

As a Group: Create one or more "recipes" for adding life to your years, and share your "ingredients." Or write your own life mission statement about the life you seek to live and what you hope to accomplish. Share your mission statement and explain its significance.

At Home: Reflect on your life, your relationships, and your accomplishments. What changes would you like to make? With what are you most pleased or hopeful?

Prayer: *Dear God, thank you for the gift of life. Help us continue to build a healthy relationship with you and with others. May we put our hope in the power of your grace and love in order to live a better life. Amen.*

4. Lord, Give Me Hope

Snapshot Summary

This chapter illustrates why our hope is in God and God's perfect love. Hope comes from God's amazing grace.

Reflection/Discussion Questions

1. Share a time when you missed an opportunity by waiting too long.
2. Reflect on/discuss the potential harm in waiting for the perfect situation or moment.
3. Is perfection an illusion? Give reasons for your answer.
4. Reflect on/discuss reasons why people often insist on searching for the perfect moment or opportunity.
5. What is our hope as Christians? Where do we place our hope, and why?
6. Why do we look for and expect perfection in other people? What problems can this cause?
7. How does God view us and our imperfections?
8. Name some keys to a successful marriage—a marriage that works.
9. List things we should and should not expect from the church.
10. What additional thoughts or ideas from this chapter would you like to explore?

Activities

As a Group: Draw illustrations of *hope*. Share and explain your drawings.

At Home: Reflect on *opportunities*, past and present. Consider your hopes and expectations as you focus this week on looking ahead and on building a stronger life and relationship with God.

Prayer: *Dear God, thank you for loving us just as we are, imperfections and all. Help us love others in the same manner. Grant us the courage to act on opportunities rather than to let them pass us by. Amen.*

5. Lord, Give Me Your Love

Snapshot Summary

This chapter explores God's love for us and reminds us of the importance of loving others.

Reflection/Discussion Questions

1. Share your favorite Bible verse and explain why it is your favorite.
2. Reflect on/discuss the depth of God's love for us. Why is it so hard to comprehend?
3. What is "the divine initiative," and why is it very important?
4. How do you respond to a love so strong that it will not let you go?
5. Reflect on/discuss the dependability of God's love and give some examples of it.
6. List some adjectives describing God's love.
7. "God's love will not let us off"; what is meant by this statement?
8. How did Jesus demonstrate God's love during his ministry? Give some examples.
9. How does God want us to respond to his love? What are we called to do?
10. What additional thoughts or ideas from this chapter would you like to explore?

Activities

As a Group: Locate examples in the Bible that show God's love.

At Home: Ask for God's love each day and look for opportunities to share God's love with others.

Prayer: *Dear God, thank you for your powerful love that will not let us go. Your love is so dependable, it is beyond our comprehension. May we show your love to others as we seek to do your will. Amen.*

6. Lord, Give Me Grace

Snapshot Summary

This chapter explores the power of grace in God's forgiving love, accepting love, and empowering love.

Reflection/Discussion Questions

1. What images or thoughts come to mind when you hear the word *grace*?
2. Reflect on/discuss John Wesley's view of grace.
3. Share a time when you experienced the grace of God. How did it feel?
4. Reflect on/discuss the William and Catherine Booth story relating to God's forgiving love.
5. List some simple and practical ways of sharing forgiving love with others.
6. Reflect on/discuss the power and meaning of God's accepting love.
7. Share a time when you experienced life-changing love.
8. Reflect on/discuss the ways God's love empowers us and changes us.
9. How do we receive God's gift of grace?
10. What additional thoughts or ideas from this chapter would you like to explore?

Activities

As a Group: Use hymnals or songbooks to locate descriptions of God's grace.

At Home: Reflect on God's gift of grace to you and to others. Respond to God's grace through your words and deeds this week.

Prayer: *Dear God, thank you for the gift of grace. Help us allow your love to empower and change us. And help us practice your forgiving love with others. Amen.*

7. Lord, Give Me a Resurrection

Snapshot Summary

This chapter explores the many different ways God resurrects us from problems, feels our pain, and raises us up.

Reflection/Discussion Questions

1. Share the name of a favorite hymn or song of faith and explain why it is so special or meaningful.
2. Name some of the many problems and situations in life where God can provide resurrection now.
3. What impresses you most in the story of Jesus raising Lazarus from the grave?
4. Reflect on/discuss how God not only feels our pain but also heals our pain.
5. Share a time when you felt the presence of Jesus while you were hurting and in pain.
6. Describe some of the different ways Jesus raises people up. How has Jesus raised you up?
7. How can we raise up other people? Give some examples.
8. Reflect on/discuss how Jesus heals, and how he often involves us in the process.
9. How do we receive the resurrection power of Jesus?
10. What additional thoughts or ideas from this chapter would you like to explore?

Activities

As a Group: Use newspapers, magazines, or the Internet to identify some of the many kinds of people in need of a resurrection. Create a list of these individuals and pray for them, asking God to resurrect them.

At Home: Reflect upon the times when God has resurrected you and given you new life. Respond with a prayer of thanks.

Prayer: *Dear God, thank you for constantly resurrecting us and our troubled world. Thank you for feeling our pain and also healing it. Show us how to raise people up to new life, in your name. Amen.*

8. Lord, Give Me Your Spirit

Snapshot Summary

This chapter explores the four gifts of the Holy Spirit and shows us how the Holy Spirit can empower us and bring us to new life.

Reflection/Discussion Questions

1. Reflect on/discuss the arrival of the Holy Spirit and how it changed the disciples.
2. What is your personal experience of the Holy Spirit? If possible, share a time when you felt the presence of the Holy Spirit.
3. List some of the times and situations in life where we need to feel God's presence.
4. Reflect on/discuss how the Holy Spirit is also a gift of pulse that brings life.

5. Our purpose is to be Christ's witnesses. How does the Holy Spirit help us accomplish this task?
6. Reflect on/discuss how the Apostle Peter is an example of the power of the Spirit in a life.
7. What types of power does the Holy Spirit provide for us today?
8. List some of the ways the Holy Spirit helps us every day and in every situation.
9. What do we need to do in order to receive the gifts of the Holy Spirit?
10. What additional thoughts or ideas from this chapter would you like to explore?

Activities

As a Group: Our mission is to be witnesses for Christ. Write a brief mission statement about this in your own words. Share your statement.

At Home: Seek the help of the Holy Spirit this week in all situations and remember the Holy Spirit is with you.

Prayer: *Dear God, thank you for the gift of the Holy Spirit. Help us be more effective witnesses for you and rely on the power of the Spirit in all situations. Amen.*

9. Lord, Give Me a Sense of Urgency

Snapshot Summary

This chapter reminds us not to hesitate in doing the work of the Lord, in loving others, and in fixing any broken relationships.

Reflection/Discussion Questions

1. Share a time when you felt a sense of urgency.
2. Give some of the reasons why people procrastinate.

3. Reflect on/discuss some of the damage caused when people wait too long before acting.
4. When is waiting a good idea? When is waiting *not* a good idea? Give examples of each situation and provide some guidelines for deciding on whether to wait.
5. Reflect on/discuss the Apostle Paul's request for Timothy to visit him.
6. How did Jesus demonstrate a sense of urgency in his ministry?
7. Why is it an urgent matter to fix broken relationships? How can this be accomplished? List some steps.
8. Name some reasons why people fail to tell others of their love.
9. How and why do we hesitate to accept God's gracious gifts?
10. What additional thoughts or ideas from this chapter would you like to explore?

Activities

As a Group: Create your own to-do lists containing three urgent tasks that need to be done. Share your priorities with your group.

At home: Examine your life and your relationships for situations that need your urgent action. Move forward this week on the most urgent need.

Prayer: *Dear God, thank you for making us an urgent priority. Help us sort through the many opportunities before us and act on those that are most important. May we not hesitate to heal relationships and care for the needs of others. Amen.*

10. Lord, Give Me Healing

Snapshot Summary

This chapter examines the gift of healing and how we can use it to heal and comfort others who exist in a world of pain.

Reflection/Discussion Questions

1. Share an experience that left you "walking but wounded."
2. List some of the reasons people get hurt or wounded.
3. Reflect on/discuss the importance of accepting the reality of our wounds. How is this accomplished?
4. Name some ways in which God provides us with power, strength, and healing.
5. How are hope and healing related?
6. Reflect on/discuss different types of healing communities. Why are they beneficial?
7. How do we become wounded healers? How can we help others?
8. What lessons about healing can we learn from the ministry of Jesus?
9. Reflect on/discuss the importance of being needed by others. How is it related to healing?
10. What additional thoughts or ideas from this chapter would you like to explore?

Activities

As a Group: Come up with ten items you would place inside a "spiritual first-aid kit" for healing the pains in life. Talk about the items in your kit and then give reasons for their inclusion.

At Home: Assume the role of a healer this week and look for opportunities to soothe the pains of others.

Prayer: *Dear God, thank you for healing us in times of need and for empowering us to heal others. Help us continue to care for those who are sick, those who are wounded, those who are lonely, and those who are dying. Amen.*

11. Lord, Give Me Childlikeness

Snapshot Summary

This chapter offers encouragement for adults to act more like children in their approach and attitude toward life.

Reflection/Discussion Questions

1. Share an activity you enjoyed as a child.
2. Describe some lessons that adults can learn from children.
3. Reflect on/discuss the ways children celebrate and embrace life. Give some examples.
4. Why do we lose our childlikeness as we grow older?
5. Reflect on/discuss the kind of approach and attitude children have toward life.
6. What do you admire most about children?
7. Why are children more trusting than adults?
8. Brainstorm ways we can become more childlike.
9. List some of the benefits of being more childlike in our lives and in our faith.
10. What additional thoughts and ideas from this chapter would you like to explore?

Activities

As a Group: Draw illustrations of heaven as a playground for people of all ages. Or briefly turn back the clock and play a children's game together.

At Home: Reflect on and identify some childlike qualities that are missing from your life. Try to recapture them.

Prayer: *Dear God, thank you for reminding us that we can be like children again. Help us celebrate and embrace life like a child and be more trusting of others. Show us all how to play well with others. Amen.*

12. Lord, Give Me Compassion

Snapshot Summary

This chapter examines our need for compassion, reconciliation, healing, and the redeeming love of Christ.

Reflection/Discussion Questions

1. Share a time when you were either the giver or the receiver of compassion.
2. In your own words, explain what it means to be a compassionate person.
3. How does a person become compassionate? What is a good starting point?
4. Name some lessons about compassion that we can learn from the ministry of Jesus.
5. Give some examples of the healing power of compassion.
6. Name some times in life when we need reconciliation, and how compassion can help.
7. What is needed in order to receive the redeeming love of Christ?
8. Name some types of people who are in special need of compassion.
9. Brainstorm some simple ways to become and act more compassionate.
10. What additional thoughts or ideas from this chapter would you like to explore?

Activities

As a Group: Hold a graduation party to observe the completion of this small-group study.

OR

As a Group: Think about this question: *What does compassion look like?* Describe or illustrate a face of compassion.

At Home: Look for opportunities to perform acts of compassion this week.

Prayer: *Dear God, thank you for reminding us of the importance of being and acting as compassionate Christians. Help us love and care for others as you love and care for us. Amen.*